GETTING UNDRESSED

– FROM PARALYSIS TO PURPOSE –

GETTING UNDRESSED

– FROM PARALYSIS TO PURPOSE –

DAVID COOKS

with Eric Wolffersdorff

HenschelHAUS
Milwaukee, Wisconsin

Published by
HenschelHAUS Publishing, Inc.
www.henschelHAUSbooks.com

Please contact the publisher for more information about special discounts for
bulk purchases. (414) 486-0653. We would be happy to customize books for
your organization or event.

ISBN: 978159598-660-3
E-ISBN: 978159598-661-0
AUDIO: 978159598-662-7
LCCN: 2018948001

Publisher's Cataloging-In-Publication Data
(Prepared by The Donohue Group, Inc.)

Names: Cooks, David. | Wolffersdorff, Eric.
Title: Getting undressed : from paralysis to purpose / David Cooks, with Eric
Wolffersdorff.
Description: Milwaukee, Wisconsin : HenschelHaus, [2018]
Identifiers: ISBN 9781595986603 | ISBN 9781595986610 (ebook)
Subjects: LCSH: Cooks, David. | Paraplegics--United States--Biography. |
African American basketball coaches--United States--Biography. | Motivation
(Psychology) | LCGFT: Autobiographies.
Classification: LCC RC406.P3 C66 2018 (print) | LCC RC406.P3 (ebook) |
DDC 362.43092--dc23

Cover design by 99designs

In loving Memory of Tyler Victor Ugolyn
(8/7/1976 - 9/11/2001)

Yesterday was History,
Tomorrow is a Mystery,
Today is a Gift from God.

"I just love playing the game."

TABLE OF CONTENTS

Acknowledgments

To my parents, Jesse and Cremella Cooks, who taught all of their four children to never quit or make excuses: You taught us about the courage to love and the power of perseverance, persistence and prayer. #Legacy

To my wife, MariPat, who believed in me and this book from the very beginning: Your unconditional love for me has made me a better person. Thank you for supporting me as I pursue my purpose. #Agape

To Eric Wolffersdorff, whose help and guidance made *Getting Undressed* possible: I couldn't have done this without you. Thank you for keeping me on task. And to Lesley DeMartini for your invaluable assistance.

To all the players who called me "coach" over the years: I wouldn't and I couldn't be a coach without you. Your impact on my life is immeasurable.

To the following coaches, athletic directors and administrators who were instrumental in providing opportunities for me to follow my passion: Will Allen, Tommy Amaker, Rev. John Belmonte, S.J., Mike Brey, Mark Briggs, Shawn Cassidy, Ric Cobb, Paul Cormier, Percy Eddie, Pete Gaudet, Jim Gerard, Dan Hardwick, Rob Judson, Rob Kennedy, Mike Krzyzewski, Tim Larkin, Bill Marifky, Frank Martin, Ritchie McKay, Jim Molinari, Vito

Montelli, Jim Moriarty, Paul Noack, Neil O'Connell, Guy Rancourt, Mike Rice, David Schulz, Shaka Smart, Kurt Soderberg and David Vander Meulen.

To all my teachers, students, coworkers, friends and mentors who have supported me along my life's journey From Paralysis to Purpose: This book is our story.

Finally, to Jesus Christ: You are the air I breathe.

FOREWORD

I FIRST MET DAVID COOKS WHEN HE WAS a coach for my oldest son at Marquette University High School. I have watched him coach and mentor all three of my sons at this fine Jesuit high school here in Milwaukee.

David has made a significant impact in the development of not only my sons, but literally thousands of others who have passed through his doors. It doesn't matter your race, gender or physical challenges, His ability to leave others better than how he found them is an authentic example of servant leadership and a unique gift. *Getting Undressed* shows us what can happen when you take a break from your problems to help someone else with theirs. David shares not only his journey to discovering Purpose, but how he put Purpose into action for the benefit of others.

I think that one of the key lessons of this book is to realize that you do not have to experience a tragedy in life to make a change or a personal transformation. It is in the realization of how grateful one can be for all the blessings in our lives, the good and bad, and how to take action and make the most of our lives while we remain on this earth.

Getting Undressed is about more than overcoming physical challenges, because we all face varying, paralyzing circumstances (i.e. emotional, financial, physical, mental) in our lives that we must overcome if we are to fulfill Purpose. David shows us that no one successfully makes this journey alone; we all need help along the way.

As an accomplished basketball coach, David speaks to the roles that leadership, teamwork and communication play in experiencing success, regardless of the profession. David is a dynamic speaker and storyteller. His story is compelling. His outlook on life is inspiring. His insights are practical and life changing.

The uniqueness of David's life experiences and his ability to effectively communicate and connect with others resonate throughout the pages of *Getting Undressed.* He has the uncanny ability of taking something personal and making it memorable. This book speaks to young and old alike about the power of persistence, the power of perspective and the power of faith in making no excuses, overcoming obstacles and, ultimately, achieving success.

From the moment I met David, it was evident that faith was a significant factor in his life—and for that to not be interwoven throughout the pages of *Getting Undressed* would be disingenuous. David is not preaching theology or religion but telling his story to inspire us and to challenge us to become the best version of ourselves.

Getting Undressed is a book that will resonate with everyone from front line workers to CEOs, players to coaches and teachers to students, because we all are on a journey of discovering our Purpose—and *Getting Undressed* will inspire you to never give up the pursuit.

—Joe Sweeney, author of New York Times bestseller,
Networking is a Contact Sport

Preface

ON DECEMBER 5, 2016, I WAS ABOARD a morning flight from Milwaukee to Boston, eager to talk about overcoming obstacles to a group of banking education directors from across the United States. About an hour and a half after takeoff, I began to experience trouble breathing. Every breath was a chore for me, and for the rest of the trip I wore an oxygen mask to avoid slipping in and out of consciousness.

I never made it to the Colonnade Hotel to speak that afternoon; instead, I was transported to the emergency room at Massachusetts General Hospital, where I stayed for nearly 30 hours because there were no open beds. Doctors and nurses ran multiple tests, ultimately determining that sub-massive blood clots had developed in my lungs. This was not my first encounter with a potentially fatal diagnosis.

On October 19, 2002, a few weeks prior to officially assuming the helm as the varsity boys' basketball coach at my alma mater, Marquette University High School (MUHS), my health had declined as well. My left eye would not open; my hearing was impaired; my speech, slurred; and my consciousness, flickering.

Medical experts from Milwaukee to Chicago examined me and ran every test they could, but none could diagnose the problem. There I was, having just earned the signature opportunity of my coaching career, with a mysterious illness leaving me teetering between life and death.

To this day, doctors can't explain what plagued me in 2002—or how I miraculously recovered to perfect health by day one of tryouts. I've been blessed to overcome these obstacles and get back on the sidelines, where I do what I do best: use the game of basketball as a platform to positively impact lives.

The 2016 diagnosis was clear and reversible. As the doctors worked to break up and clear the blood clots, I shared my story with them. When I finished, the doctor turned to my wife and said, "We need to get him healthy and back on planes—back to doing what he came to Boston to do. He needs to share his story around the country. There's work he needs to finish."

The doctor then turned to me.

"Where's your book?"

I took a deep breath. "I'm thinking about writing one," I replied feebly. For years I had thought about writing my story. I wanted to tell my story, but I hadn't invested the time to actually do it. I'm not much for reading or writing.

"Well, what are you waiting for? Your story and the things you've been able to accomplish could really help others. You should really get that book written." He had struck a nerve.

With that statement, my prognosis went from life threatening to life giving. God had once again put me in contact with the right people at the right time—not only to get me back on the horse after getting knocked off, but also to affirm my purpose in life.

Now, 16 months later, I've finally completed what I wish I'd done years ago (and nearly didn't have the chance to do). Thank you, Dr. Katrina Armstrong and the Massachusetts General

Hospital staff, for nursing me back to health. But more importantly, thank you for nudging me and asking the questions I needed to
hear.

* * * * *

Regardless of race, gender, and social status, everybody gets
undressed daily. We undergo the daily ritual of casting off our old,
worn clothes and tolerate a few moments of vulnerability before
redressing and restarting the next part of the day. Getting undressed represents change and transition: It's an ending and a
beginning; it's rebranding. Getting undressed doesn't change who
we are, but it changes what we're about to do. What we take off
indicates where we've been, and what we put on signals where
we're going.

Getting undressed is more about choosing and preparing what
new clothes to wear—and actually putting them on—than it is about
losing your shirt. Getting undressed is something that we all must
do in order to move forward, to start over, to have a new
beginning.

And sometimes getting undressed requires a drastic change: a
radical wardrobe makeover.

As a 15-year-old high school sophomore, getting undressed
came to mean maintaining my independence and recovering my
self-esteem as I started anew after a major setback. To this day,
every day serves as a reminder of how fortunate I am to be able to
get undressed and move forward with my life. I realized this 38
years ago at Sacred Heart Rehabilitation Center, and it's still true
today.

Getting Undressed chronicles my journey through life from Paralysis to Purpose: the successes, the failures, the ups and the downs. It is not a step-by-step guidebook to overcoming life's challenges; rather, it's a narrative filled with principles, values, and skills you can apply when you have no choice but to handle them. It is my hope that *Getting Undressed* will instruct, inspire, and encourage you to continue to fight and move forward despite the obstacles you face in your life.

This is my getting undressed story: from paralysis to purpose.

—David Cooks

CHAPTER 1: PARALYSIS

A Wardrobe Malfunction

Adversity doesn't define you,
but it can influence the road you take to becoming who you are.

LIKE MANY OF THE KIDS IN MY NEIGHBORHOOD, I grew up with a love for the game of basketball. I played year-round: indoor, outdoor, recreation leagues, pick-up. Whenever I could join a game, I would. During the summer, the playgrounds were my second home. Summer was the best time to play because the Wisconsin weather cooperated, it wouldn't get dark until 9:00 p.m., and, best of all, school was out.

Growing up, my parents didn't have a lot of rules—but completing my homework before playing basketball or watching TV (or doing anything, for that matter) was one of them. The other rule was to come home once the streetlights came on. Both of these rules I followed, and they provided me with a couple of principles I live by today: 1) Do what I have to do before what I want to do, and 2) Not many good things happen after dark—except for catching catfish, of course.

My first experience with competitive basketball was in grade school with the Pro Kids basketball team. Coach Thomas Hines was my first head coach. He was enthusiastic, an excellent strategist, and demanding—not demeaning. But make no mistake: Coach Hines was a disciplinarian; he held each player accountable to do his job, and yes, there were consequences—running—if someone wasn't holding up his end of the bargain.

He kept things simple for us, but it was clear he had a complex understanding of how the game should be played. More important, he understood that basketball was more than just an exercise in X's and O's. It was personal—it was about relationships; it was about people. It required individuals from all different walks of life, with different levels of ability and motivation, to work together toward a common goal.

Coach Hines was the first person to not only recognize my potential as a basketball player, but to actually pull me aside and tell me. Throughout grade school and middle school, he inspired me to work hard and uncover ways to get better every day. He didn't just care about me as a point guard on the floor, responsible for orchestrating the offense, but he also cared about me conducting a plan for my life off the floor.

Having grown up in the projects, I encountered my fair share of distractions and non-examples of getting it done. But through the loving guidance of my parents and the constant vigilance of Coach Hines, I was able to avoid the three D's—drinking, drugs and dice—while taking care of my business in the classroom.

By the time I reached high school, my friends gave me the nickname "Gus," after Gus Williams, the point guard for the Seattle Supersonics. I wasn't very big and wasn't that athletic, but my ability to pass and find the open man in traffic was my trademark. My friends and I would play during lunch, when the gym was open. It wasn't always the prettiest basketball, but that didn't matter. I was doing what I loved.

My freshman year goal was simple: to make one of the two freshman teams at MUHS. The idea was simple enough—but with over 80 people turning out for tryouts that first day, I knew it wouldn't be easy. Nonetheless, I felt good about my chances.

I made it through the first two days without getting cut. After day three, the coaches told me that I didn't make the freshman "A" team, but that I hadn't been cut from the program. I was relieved knowing that I was still "on the board." Making a team—even the freshman "B" team—was still my goal.

On the final day of tryouts, I was participating in a full court drill when I felt a tug in my right hip, forcing me to pull up lame. I hobbled to the sidelines and sat out for the rest of tryouts. I wanted to practice, show everyone my skills and make a positive last impression, but my hip refused.

I didn't make the "B" team either. I was disappointed, but not discouraged. Next year.

Fast forward to my sophomore year. I spent all offseason getting bigger, stronger, faster and more skilled. I played and played and played against the best competition I could find, so I could prove to the coaches that they made a mistake in cutting me from the basketball program as a freshman. My high school team was good—like winning state good—and I wanted to be part of the team that could deliver a basketball State Championship to the school. As junior varsity tryouts approached, I was ready—mentally and physically.

On the morning of Friday, October 19, 1979, a few days before tryouts, I woke up with some pain in my back and soreness in my legs. Athletes can relate. We're used to the nicks and bruises, let alone a little soreness, that come with playing sports. Nothing I couldn't handle. I showered, made some breakfast, packed my basketball shoes and shorts, and was off to school.

That day, we had our first quarter exams. It meant we only had to be there for the morning and could leave once exams ended. I, however, had intentions of staying after school to scrimmage during the open gym session that followed the exams. The coaches would be there. I missed out on the team last year, so I knew I had to impress the coaches enough to earn a spot this year.

But as I played that afternoon, I wasn't "wizarding" my way around defenders like I normally could. Every movement—even basic maneuvers—required a little more effort and attention. I didn't have the normal spring to my step that made me a lethal player, with or without the ball in my hands.

This didn't stop me from playing, though; in fact, it motivated me to work harder, even as my body resisted with every cut and jump. Of all the days to sleep funny or twist a muscle in my back, it had to be the day the JV and Varsity coaches were in attendance.

This wasn't going as planned.

The open gym ended, and—a bit dejected—I left the gym and hopped on the city bus to head home. The discomfort wasn't going away. The ache in my back now ran down my right leg, and by the time I got home, even my mom noticed I was limping.

"Just a little sore. I'll be fine," I reassured her as I opened the basement door and headed downstairs to sprawl on the couch and watch TV.

PARALYSIS

A little later, the phone rang. Probably for me: maybe my girlfriend, maybe some other girl. Like any teenage boy who has discovered girls, I was eager to get to the phone upstairs. But what happened next scared me. I bounced off the couch and attempted to get up the stairs, but my legs weren't cooperating. I really struggled to get to the phone, only to hear a dial tone. My disappointment about missing the call was short lived, as I realized that perhaps something was really wrong.

I told my parents what happened, and we did what we always did when someone in the family faced a problem: we prayed.

"Are you sure you're okay?" my mom asked.

"I'm okay," I said. "I'm going to take a nap. I'll be fine when I get up."

I limped off to my room to take a nap, hoping that by the time I woke up I'd feel refreshed, recharged and ready to start my weekend.

That didn't happen.

I woke up feeling worse. When I tried to get out of bed, my legs couldn't hold the weight of my body and I nearly collapsed. Bracing myself up on the side table next to my bed, I called for my parents. They must have sensed the panic in my voice, because they came running to my room. I told them what happened. Using the walls for support, I was able to walk—but it was a labor to do so. My father and I left for the emergency room at St. Michael's Hospital, while my mother stayed home with my siblings.

We sat in the waiting room for what seemed like an eternity. During those five hours of waiting, my condition continued to worsen. By this point, I needed a wheelchair to get around.

When they finally brought me to the examination room, the physician asked me question after question, feeling his way up and down my body in his search for the cause of my problems. He stuck pins and needles into my lower body, but I didn't grimace or scowl as each point penetrated my skin.

I didn't feel a thing.

I couldn't imagine what was wrong. Did my injury freshman year have anything to do with this? Did I aggravate something in my preparation for the upcoming basketball season? Just a week earlier, my doctor had given me a clean bill of health. What could have happened over seven days? For the first time, I was really concerned that there was something really wrong. Something serious.

Eventually, I was taken into a larger room with more specialized and technical equipment. I lay on my belly and was strapped to a CT scanning machine for a myelogram, where a contrast dye was injected into my spinal column to see if they could rule out or confirm anything neurological. The x-ray table tilted so the dye could spread up and down my spinal cord. I turned my head, looking at the little screen, not really knowing what to expect. All of a sudden, the dye stopped and pooled.

"Yep, that's it alright," the physician said gravely.

The physicians ran a few more tests and determined that a blood vessel had erupted on my spine. I was transferred once more to a different unit, where a team of surgeons—some of Milwaukee's best—performed immediate exploratory surgery to see if there was something they could do to release the blockage. Unfortunately, the damage had already been done. In less than 24 hours, my life had been turned upside down.

Paralysis

No grand event. No gruesome collision. Nothing caught on camera to show my family and friends. "The event," as I now call it, wasn't really an event at all—yet it left me largely immobile from my diaphragm down to my feet. I had pretty good use of my arms, but nothing but a few tingling sensations in my legs. All the things I used to be able to do instinctively, I now needed to do in a wheelchair.

A spinal aneurysm had left me a T-6 paraplegic.

Chapter 2: Perspective

Starting Over

How you see it will determine how you attack it.

PARALYSIS CAN TAKE ON MANY FORMS. It can be emotional, psychological and/or spiritual. For me, it happened to be physical. At its wickedest, paralysis has the power to lead to emotional, psychological, spiritual, and even physical death. Remaining in the place we've been hurt, offended, disappointed or discouraged only strengthens paralysis' grip, which can lead to additional paralysis that affects one's quality of life.

Regardless of its impact or manifestation, moving forward from paralysis to purpose is something every human being can and must do. It was something I needed to do as well.

I stayed in the hospital for a few days following my surgery before they transported me to the Sacred Heart Rehabilitation Center to begin occupational and physical therapy. My family and I had to learn what to do next, how to get me back home and back to school, and how to make this all work.

The ride to the rehab center was a bumpy one. Everything was moving so fast. Everything was foreign and new to me. I didn't have time to think about all that had happened and changed in the last 72 hours. As we hit another pothole, an EMT aboard told me that I had a long road ahead. He estimated it would be about six months of rehab before I could go home.

Six months? I thought. Man, I'm not going to take that long. I don't have that kind of time. I need to get back to school. That's way too long. Seriously? It may take some time, but not that long to get back on my feet. Will it?

We arrived at the rehabilitation center and I was taken to my room, where I met my roommate—Tony Otters, a quadriplegic a little older than me from Oconomowoc, Wisconsin. He was sitting up in his wheelchair—something I had yet to do. I hadn't even gotten out of a bed. I hadn't even changed from my hospital gown into normal clothes.

Tony had been injured in a diving accident a few months prior to my arrival at Sacred Heart, but his outlook on life was just what I needed. Despite his physical paralysis, Tony thought and talked differently from what I thought most people would in his situation. He never complained, though no one would blame him if he did. He was optimistic about his future. He was enthusiastic about going home soon. He was doing whatever he could on his own; but for the things he couldn't do, he gladly accepted help instead of wallowing in negativity or stubbornness.

But his dreams didn't stop there. He was planning on going to college and becoming a physician. Like Coach Hines, Tony inspired me to be upbeat, to work hard, to focus on my abilities, and to not let paralysis beat me. Life didn't end just because we lost the use of some of our limbs.

Because of Tony, and along with him, I refused to accept the narrative that my situation dictated my fate. Together on our wing at Sacred Heart, this white kid from a wealthy suburb of Milwaukee and a black kid from the projects pushed each other toward our goals of getting better, finding victories in every moment, and learning how to be independent and productive.

Tony inspired me. What were the odds that of all the patients at the hospital, Tony was situated next to me? I saw Tony, the medicine, the doctors and the rehab as just another expression of God's grace.

One of my first group meetings was with a collection of physicians and therapists on a different wing of the building. I was lifted from my bed and into a Cadillac-style chair, like a lazy-boy on coasters, on which I was pushed down a bunch of hallways. I had no idea where I was going, and it didn't help that all the walls were painted the same. I caught glimpses of people in the rooms I passed, and these passing glances forever changed my perspective about my situation. I saw people, both older and younger than me, sitting in wheelchairs with no use of their arms or legs, nodding their heads or blowing into tubes to communicate the simplest of messages. I saw people with brain injuries dealing with memory loss—perhaps people who suffered strokes. I saw people who needed the assistance of machines simply to breathe. It went on and on and on.

My mouth hung open in disbelief. The number of patients suffering from fates far worse than mine staggered me. I had no idea how prevalent this problem was. And these were only the people from the greater Milwaukee area! Imagine the number of people across the state, the country and the world! I finally understood that what I had to deal with was not that bad. I was blessed to be as well off as I was. For the first time since my diagnosis, it wasn't about me.

The meeting began with a review of my diagnosis, which quickly transitioned to their prognosis—a laundry list of things I "would never be able to do again."

"You won't ever be able to walk again..."

"Or ever play basketball again..."

"Or be fully independent again..."

"Or—"

"Whoa, whoa, whoa."

I had to stop them. I was a basketball player; I was competitive. After what I had just witnessed in the hallways, I refused to blow my situation—my circumstances—out of proportion. Here I was trying to figure out what was going on and how I could get back to school, catch up on my homework and move my life forward, and these doctors were double-teaming me in the corner about everything I won't be able to do once I leave the hospital.

I asked, "Is there anything I will be able to do?"

I had caught them off guard—but I wasn't interested in, nor did I have time for, impossibilities—only possibilities. What could I do? What were the possibilities that were still available to me? How could I maximize what I had left?

I didn't view this wheelchair thing as a permanent situation. (I still don't.) Yes, I was coming to understand the daily challenges I would face in my life until I got back on my feet; but this would not control or rule the rest of my life. Not in my mind. I still had the right to live a full life.

Instead of commending my positivity, though, they thought I was in denial. They thought I needed to see a psychiatrist. I wasn't depressed, or angry, or discouraged—but the physicians and therapists couldn't comprehend how I could be at peace so quickly after the world as I knew it had been turned upside down.

Nonetheless, I played their game and saw a psychiatrist (like I had a choice in the matter). The report came back that I wasn't depressed, I wasn't angry, and I was perfectly in touch with reality. My therapy would begin the next day.

Learning how to function without the use of my legs posed some serious challenges for me. Relatively speaking, not walking was the easy part of the deal. Potty training myself was a different story. At 15, I had to figure out a new way of going to the bathroom. I had to figure out how to read my body and relearn how to use the facilities so I wouldn't wet or soil myself...and it was disgusting. It was embarrassing, but I was not embarrassed. It was irritating, but I was not irritated. I credit the therapists and nurses who helped me get through this process with a sense of dignity, pride, and understanding.

There were two types of therapy I needed to begin: occupational therapy and physical therapy. Occupational therapy focused on developing my motor skills, thinking skills and practical daily life skills. Largely, I had fun in occupational therapy—putting square pegs in square holes, making pizza, putting together puzzles and squeezing handgrips. The same could not be said for physical therapy.

Physical therapy was five days a week and four to six hours per day. It focused heavily on making transfers—like getting out of bed, into and out of a chair, a car, and so on—and building strength to successfully make those transfers. It was intense—as intense as the wind sprints Coach Hines made us do. There was no way I could see myself doing this for six whole months.

However, there was one thing I really looked forward to doing while in physical therapy: getting behind the wheel of a yellow AMC Pacer—"The Fishbowl." The Pacer may be one of the ugliest cars ever made, but if it could help me drive, it was a Rolls Royce as far as I was concerned. Driving, though, had to take a back seat to other more pressing daily tasks first—like getting dressed.

Learning to get dressed was by far the highlight of my physical therapy experience and my most meaningful accomplishment. I started by learning how to get dressed on the mat with the help of the therapists. With them doing most of the work, everything was quick and smooth. I knew I'd have to be able to dress myself alone—and soon, if I wanted to spend a weekend away from the rehab center, much less be discharged upon mastering this task.

Using some pillows, I propped myself up in the bed to help maintain my balance, because my core and back muscles weren't strong enough yet. Sitting cross-legged, I put on one sock and one pants leg first, careful not to pull the pant leg above my knee, and then straightened that leg out a little. Then I repeated the same process with the other leg so all I needed to do was pull the pants up. I then removed the pillows to lie flat on the bed. Next, I rolled from side to side, shifting my weight enough to allow me to pull my pants all the way up. The first time took me an hour, but over time I became quite good at getting dressed; I could even begin the process in my wheelchair before transferring to the bed for the final steps.

But getting undressed? That was something else entirely.

I wasn't sure why, but I hadn't learned or practiced getting undressed during a physical therapy session. For a while, every night I'd have one of the nurses help me get undressed and ready for bed. A few weeks into my stay, there came a night where I waited and waited and waited, but no nurse showed up. It was a busy night with a lot of commotion in the hallways and several "code calls" over the intercom. With no one to help me, I was left with the choice of sleeping in my clothes or getting undressed and ready for bed. I chose the latter.

First, I tried to do the reverse of what I did to put my clothes on—but that didn't work. I wound up wasting nearly an hour sitting cross-legged, rolling from side-to-side and getting nothing accomplished. Back in the wheelchair I went. I considered waiting for a nurse. I was tired. I was frustrated. It would have been a lot easier just to wait for help and figure it out a different day.

As I sat there, though, my mind went to work. There had to be a way to get these pants and shoes off—even from the wheelchair. I wanted to prove to myself that I could do it, because I really wanted to get home. I didn't want a nurse to come anymore. I no longer wanted to rely on the nurses to help me get undressed and ready for bed.

I tried again. I locked my wheelchair in place and pushed up on the armrest, just high enough to pull my pants down with my other hand. I alternated this process until my pants were at my knees. I could then take one leg and cross it on top of the other leg, remove my shoe and pants from that leg, and repeat it with the other leg.

Mission accomplished. I was one night closer to sleeping in my own bed.

The hectic night and the nurses' absence was all a blessing in disguise. Besides, the nurses' assistance was never meant to be permanent—only a stopgap until I could do it alone. The idea of getting home fueled me to continue to adjust my perspective about my circumstances. Thinking outside of the box was necessary in order for me to solve that night's dilemma. The need to get undressed wasn't really a problem or an obstacle; it was an opportunity for me to grow and build confidence.

Like I told the physicians and therapists at my first meeting, I was only interested in what I could do, not what I could not do. I learned quickly that daily challenges are the norm when using a wheelchair. But every day can also bring victory.

My story was just beginning. My purpose, my passion and my resolve were never paralyzed. I just needed to figure out innovative ways to pursue and reach my goals.

On December 24, 1979, I was discharged from Sacred Heart Rehabilitation Center—four months ahead of schedule.

Chapter 3: Priorities

Making Things Work

Excuses don't stop you.
Obstacles don't stop you. Stopping stops you.

When I was nine years old, my family moved from the Northlawn Projects to a home on 24th Street, a whopping three blocks away. But moving—no matter the distance—was a big deal for us. Our modest, classic-style, two-story, Lannon-stone bungalow was nestled in a dead-end street adjacent to Lincoln Creek Parkway and a block away from St. Michael's Hospital. No white picket fence or sprawling backyard, but it was our home—a place where we bonded as a family, and a place I valued even more after two months in a rehabilitation hospital.

Returning home on Christmas Eve was one of the most exciting days of my life, but it also presented a series of challenges. I was returning to a home that wasn't made for someone in a wheelchair. Steps leading to the front and back doors would make it difficult for me to enter and leave. The back door would provide the easiest entryway—one step up to get into the house and three more steps up to reach the main floor. No ramps. No automatic doors. My parents and siblings would have to tip my wheelchair back into a wheelie to get me up and down the stairs to get me in and out of the house. It wasn't ideal, but we'd have to make it work.

Inside, it wasn't exactly the "open concept" floor design you see on HGTV—but my family worked hard to make our home as wheelchair-accessible as possible. Dana, my oldest sister, gave up her room on the first floor of the house, since I could no longer access mine. In exchange, they converted the upstairs attic into a bedroom for Dana and my younger sister, Anna. My bedroom had been upstairs, and the last time I saw it was on October 19, 1979.

Before the spinal aneurysm, I shared my bedroom with my older brother, William, who was a senior in high school. My sloppiness irritated him; his neatness irritated me. I remember how we used to have an imaginary line in our room that I couldn't cross unless I was putting the white rectangular fan in the window.

My "side" of the room was closest to the door leading downstairs. William occupied the window side of the room. First-born privileges, I guess. I had to steer clear of all of his stuff. I couldn't touch any of it—especially his boom box stereo with a cassette player. However, I constantly reminded him that he had to step across the line to my side in order to leave the room. Advantage me.

Our relationship was classic. We fought and argued like brothers, but we knew we had each other's backs when it counted—and we had great times in that room. Our new living arrangements meant no more brother-to-brother fireside chats late at night, no more staying up until the wee hours of the morning listening to music or just screwing around together. In those moments, our imaginary line was more imaginary than it was a line.

My first night back, we ordered pizza from Pasquale's, a favorite of mine. It was my first family dinner in a long time. It was so good to be with them again, but that day was physically and emotionally draining. I made my way to my new bedroom and successfully undressed myself for bed.

The next day was Christmas Day.

Despite having Christmas fever, it took me a little while to get ready the following morning. At Sacred Heart, everything was set up specifically to meet my needs. Here, I had to adjust to the bed height, the bathroom size—everything. Welcome to the real world. It was like squeezing those square pegs into round holes. I could barely fit into the bathroom and had trouble closing the door. There was no roll-in shower, no shower bench, and all we had was a tub and showerhead. Somehow, I had to lift myself in and out of the tub—something I hadn't experienced or practiced at Sacred Heart.

If this was going to work, I knew I couldn't do it alone. I don't believe in the narrative of pulling oneself up by the bootstraps, as that only causes groin pains. No one reaches goals in isolation. But then again, depending on others for so many things was something I wasn't accustomed to. Self-sufficiency was always my goal after the spinal aneurysm. I wanted to be as independent as possible, knowing that the spontaneity in my life was all but gone. I never foresaw needing assistance long term. I opposed receiving help—especially from the government—for anything I could do for myself.

That Christmas morning, however, I needed help—so I asked my parents. I knew I would need to get more comfortable asking others for help when I needed it. This was difficult for me...at first. I later realized that if I could make my life easier and chose not to, I'd be the fool.

We all gathered as a family around the Christmas tree in the living room, with the smell of coffee and bacon emanating from the kitchen. We all took turns reading the Biblical account of the birth of Jesus in Luke's Gospel, and it wouldn't be Christmas at the Cooks' house if Mahalia Jackson's Christmas album wasn't playing in the background. My dad loved that album and would put the record on repeat to play it over and over again: "Silent Night." "Hark! The Harold Angels Sing." "Go Tell It On the Mountain." Christmas was very Christ-centered in our home. No "Grandma Got Run Over By a Reindeer" or "Santa Claus is Coming to Town." Only side A and B of Mahalia Jackson's album—all day long.

There weren't a lot of gifts under the tree that year. My homecoming was the best Christmas gift for my family and me— especially considering the extra accommodations my parents made for me while maintaining a home and parenting my other siblings. I can't imagine how stressful that must have been.

Most of their efforts went towards Christmas dinner, and it did not disappoint. Ham, turkey, collard greens, dressing, macaroni and cheese, green beans, mashed potatoes, sweet potato pies, pound cake, and my dad's favorite—strawberry pecan cake—filled our dining room table and any free counter space in the kitchen. Imagining this yearly spread motivated me to work extra hard those last few weeks at the rehabilitation hospital. After a couple months of eating hospital food, having home-cooked meals—especially Christmas dinner—was a delicacy. And to spend it with family made the occasion that much more satisfying. We ate until we were content.

Returning home in a wheelchair didn't just change my life, it changed all of our lives—and for the better. It made me realize that life wouldn't stop and wait for my family or me because I was in a wheelchair. And it shouldn't.

Obstacles only change the direction we must take to reach our goals; they don't change our goals. Since my goal was important, I needed to find solutions around my obstacles. I had to embrace the challenges and realize that they're vital ingredients in the recipe for success. At the end of the day, I still needed to get the job done—and returning to school was an important first step. Within about a week, I was to return to MUHS.

Getting a quality education was the number one priority in our home. My family didn't have much growing up, but I didn't know that. If we were poor, I never knew it. There was always enough, but no extra. PF Flyer sneakers and shopping at Goodwill kept us clothed, and powdered milk, generic food and water in the ketchup bottle were commonplace in our kitchen.

My parents, who migrated to the north from the oppression of Jim Crow in the South, made incredible sacrifices to provide a private school education from kindergarten through high school for my siblings and me. Good grades and good behavior were expected in our home, and those expectations didn't change for me now that I was in a wheelchair. Excuses weren't part of the equation, and that included racism or any other injustice that crossed our paths. We were always told that education, especially reading, was the key that would open the door to countless possibilities. An education beyond high school, something neither of my parents had, was the endgame for us.

Graduating with my high school class was a concern of mine as I prepared to return to school. I had my work cut out for me to get caught up with my coursework and maintain my excellent grades, because my parents' standards for me would remain the same. Their expectations were high. They expected me to be excellent in whatever I did—no excuses, no exceptions. And I came to expect it, too.

The day of returning to school had finally arrived. I was nervous. I was excited. I missed my friends. It was like being a freshman all over again—of course, with a few changes this time around. And by the way, I missed basketball, too.

I sat in the kitchen, looking out the alley window and waiting for my ride. I wouldn't be taking the city bus to school anymore. At that time, many of the mandated public accommodations for people with disabilities—including curb cuts, wheelchair lifts, etc.— were not mainstream yet. Slushy Wisconsin winters also made it impractical and unsafe for me to slog to the nearest city bus stop.

I waited for Care Cab, a transportation company, to arrive to take me to school. I pondered what going back to school would be like. How would I get in the building? How would I get to the cafeteria? The bathroom? The fourth floor? As far as I could remember, there were stairs everywhere.

When Care Cab finally arrived, it wasn't at all what I expected. Parked in the alley was a rusting Carolina-blue station wagon with wood paneling on its sides. The driver exited the car and made his way to the back door of our house. He seemed like a nice guy, but his appearance wasn't so nice. He looked disheveled, was poorly dressed, and overweight. His reddish-blond hair and beard weren't groomed. I wasn't sure what was worse, his appearance or the vile feet-and-Fritos odor that sprang from the car when he opened the door. His nickname amongst my peers later became Pigpen, after the Charlie Brown character.

Getting picked up and dropped off from school was normal for 15-year-olds, but so was being self-conscious. I couldn't believe I had to be dropped off in an old-school station wagon with a smelly driver. But despite my first impression, my driver was reliable and passionate about his job. He was always on time. He always helped get me in and out of my home. He always made sure I made it safely into school. It was an early lesson on the importance of ability versus identity. His appearance was no indication of the work he did, nor of the impact he'd have in helping me get back into the mainstream. I wanted others to see me for who I was and not the wheelchair I was in, so who was I to judge another based on similar criterion?

That first ride to school was a bumpy one, but I made it. My first day of high school in a wheelchair was about to begin.

Chapter 4: Perseverance

Friends Matter

Persevering through life's challenges sometimes requires getting help. You're not in it all by yourself.

THE CARE CAB PARKED IN THE ALLEY outside a gray door. I was met by Mr. Snopek, head of the maintenance department at Marquette High School. He opened the door to the loading dock, which was a dark, cluttered obstacle course lined with snowblowers, landscaping equipment, power tools, and whatever else the school needed to spruce itself up. At the end of the loading dock was the freight elevator that must have come with the school when it first opened in 1857. This elevator wasn't an elevator I was used to; it reminded me of the ones I saw in early 20th-century black-and-white films—only without the elevator operator.

To get on the elevator, we lifted the wooden and metal gates and climbed aboard. Mr. Snopek closed the gates behind us and then proceeded to close the glass doors and metal gate in front of us. There were no buttons, no keys, no emergency call buttons. This was the kind of hand-operated elevator where if you got lucky, there'd be no step up when you stopped the elevator and opened the doors. Otherwise, it was back to square one.

Welcome to accessibility in 1980.

Like our home, Marquette High was not as wheelchair friendly as Sacred Heart. But what places were? Sacred Heart was ideal for someone recovering from a spinal cord injury with the latest resources and technology. That said, Marquette High did everything, given its structural limitations, to make it as smooth a transition for me as they possibly could. It wasn't ideal; it wasn't what I expected. But it worked, and this allowed me to continue attending Marquette High.

My first stop was the main office on the first floor.

"Welcome back, David. I'm so excited to see you," Mrs. Wilson, the school secretary, said. "I was praying for you."

"Thank you for your prayers. I'm glad to be back at school."

"Wait right here while I get Father Goetz."

Rev. Goetz, S.J. was the school principal, and when he emerged from his office, he gave me a hug and told me he had something for me. When he returned, he wheeled in a large, portable standing box.

"For you," he said. "So you can stretch your legs daily while you're here."

I hadn't seen one before, but I could figure out its use easy enough. A standing box enabled me to safely stand and support myself to allow blood circulation throughout my body. I couldn't imagine how he knew about these contraptions. Only later did I find out that he had been in contact with my therapists at Sacred Heart. They recommended that I get one so my blood wouldn't pool. But Rev. Goetz didn't buy one; he made one.

Besides preaching the Word of God, Rev. Goetz was somewhat of an engineer and carpenter. He built the standing box for me because he knew the financial strain my family was under after our increased medical expenses. He handed me paperwork from the government, stating that it met all the safety and structural requirements they mandated. This was the first of many random acts of kindness that the people at MUHS gave my family and me over the next two and a half years.

From there, Mr. Chaney, Dean of Students, accompanied me to my new locker on the first floor—another accommodation the school made for me, since my old locker on the fourth floor was out of the question (the elevator didn't go up that far). He also gave me a modified class schedule with none of my classes on the fourth floor. I still had a few important questions, though.

"Where's the bathroom?"

Mr. Chaney took me around the corner to a faculty restroom— a single, gender-neutral bathroom with grab bars, spacious enough for me to maneuver my wheelchair without any restrictions. I breathed a sigh of relief.

"How do I get downstairs to the cafeteria? Or to the Blue and Gold Room?"

Those would be a challenge.

The elevator let us off in the basement in front of a heavy steel gray door. There was very little room for me to negotiate the door with the wheelchair, but I managed. On the other side of the door was a tunnel, not the hallway I was accustomed to using when heading to the cafeteria or to the Blue and Gold Room. I proceeded to move through the dimly lit tunnel and suddenly realized that I was behind the stage of the school's auditorium. The walls on both sides of the tunnel were filled with the names of actors, actresses and student productions from as far back as the 1950s.

Other than the tunnel's initial decline, the ride was smooth and had manageable turns to get to the end, where I needed some help to get up its steep incline. I never knew this tunnel existed behind the stage. In my short time back at home, and now at school, I was becoming more and more familiar with back doors, kitchens and secret, tunnel-like entrances. Although not always ideal, I was simply grateful to have ways to get where I needed to go.

The next stop after exiting the tunnel was the Blue and Gold Room, which was the home of THE WAVE, the school radio station. This was also where students were allowed to hang out during free periods throughout the day, including lunch. I was relieved that getting to the cafeteria from the Blue and Gold Room was an easy roll down the hallway and something I could do by myself.

The bell was about to ring, ending the homeroom period before the first class of the day, so we hurried back to the tunnel to take the elevator to the first floor for my first class. I tried not to show it, but I was nervous, nervous, nervous.

It's hard to describe, but the school had changed from my memory. Maybe it was because the perspective from my wheelchair made it look different. Maybe it was because I had grown too accustomed to Sacred Heart. Maybe it was because now I fully appreciated what Marquette High meant to me, having been absent from it. I had physically changed from the last time I was here, but my purpose for being there was exactly the same. I came for a college-prep education, and that's what I intended to receive.

By now, the hallways were clear of students because the first hour bell had rung. Mr. Chaney led me down the hall. The students nearest the doors we passed leaned to gaze at us as we went by. It became apparent to me that I was no longer just another student, but a student that everybody would now recognize and know.

Finally, we reached our destination. As I entered through the door, the class jumped from their seats into a standing ovation that gave me Goosebumps. From that moment on, I knew everything was going to be okay. My school community accepted me, welcomed me back, and wanted to help me transition. The smile on my face from that moment stayed all day.

I spent most of that second semester catching up academically while making necessary lifestyle changes now that I was in a wheelchair. The privileges that came with walking were no longer at my disposal. Before going anywhere, I had to call and check on accessibility. There was (and still is) nothing more stressful than having access to a building only to find out I couldn't get into certain rooms—especially the bathroom. There's a big difference between accessibility and opportunity, and they shouldn't be mutually exclusive.

The same held true if I wanted to go out with my friends. I had to go through a mental checklist every time: Who could take me places and pick me up? Would I even be able to get in the car? Would my wheelchair fit? Might I put my friends or myself in an uncomfortable situation? Having to plan ahead for nearly everything was a pretty big adjustment—and reality check—for me. But this became my new normal.

There were four classmates in particular who made my transition from a life of walking to life in a wheelchair as pleasant and productive as possible. Robert Tomlinson "R.T.", William

"Bill" Thompson, Jan Mueller and Jim Van Eerden made sure I went to school dances and sporting events, welcomed me into their homes, and included me on their social calendars.

We were an eclectic circle of friends with diverse backgrounds, personalities, political leanings, religious outlooks and economic statuses. Still, each person found his own way of confirming to me that my life wasn't over even if I'd have to spend the rest of my high school career in a wheelchair.

R.T. was a star defensive end on the football team at Marquette High School. On the field, he was competitive, tough, and had a mean streak in him. Off the field, he was one of the most compassionate people I had ever come in contact with—just a nice guy. We grew up in the same neighborhood. Like my family, his family didn't have much in terms of material things and finances. However, R.T. made sure I had what I needed. Specifically, he became the primary source of transportation to and from school-related events. He became a big brother to me in the school after my biological brother graduated and left for UW-Eau Claire. Like my brother William, R.T. looked out for me and made sure I wasn't picked on or bullied.

Jan Mueller was a devout Catholic, committed to social justice—especially in the areas of race and economics. He had an infectious smile and laugh, always upbeat and positive. He came from a family of German immigrants—Jan's father was an orthopedic surgeon who grew up in Elm Grove, a wealthy suburb of Milwaukee, but you would never know their economic profile unless you visited his house. I was a frequent guest at their elegant home, and it was an oddly wonderful experience. His family spoke German; we ate wiener schnitzel, sauerkraut and spätzle, and we celebrated German traditions with his grandmother who lived there too. They often inquired in broken English about my family, as they had an extra level of concern not just for me, but also for them. What made my relationship with Jan so special was that Jan didn't live on a one-way street. Jan was a frequent guest at our home, where we also conversed, ate and engaged in my family stories and traditions as well.

Jim Van Eerden also lived in Elm Grove, and he came from a family of Marquette High graduates. Jim's dad was a prominent businessman in the Milwaukee community who instilled an entrepreneurial mindset in his children: They weren't afraid of failure, but more importantly, they believed in the power of possibilities. Jim and I were two devout, non-Catholic Christian students at the Catholic, Jesuit high school. He helped me find a creative way of expressing two of the most important things in my life at the time—faith and music.

Jim expanded my exposure to Contemporary Christian Music (CCM), which spanned multiple genres but primarily appealed to a white audience. I introduced him to Urban Contemporary Gospel. Together, we DJ'ed a Christian rock radio show on the THE WAVE. We combined our vinyl record collections (40 LPs) for the show, and we featured some of the pioneers in CCM—including Phil Keaggy, Andrae Crouch, Keith Greene, The Winans, Joe English, Amy Grant and Michael W. Smith. I loved doing the show, and I had a voice for radio. I wondered if I could keep doing this in college.

Bill Thompson came from a large, well-known family in the Marquette High School community. Unlike R.T., Bill didn't know me until I was in a wheelchair; we never connected until the middle of our junior year. Bill was in the same French class as I was, and he was also a lover of music—a fellow DJ on THE WAVE. Bill was a known partier and a heavy drug and alcohol user during his first three years of high school. I wasn't a partier, and to Bill, that was appealing. It was as unlikely a friendship as it could have been. Here I was trying to figure out how to live the rest of my life, and he was trying to figure out how not to waste the rest of his.

Our common ground came in the form of music—specifically Bob Dylan. Bill was a huge Dylan fan who enjoyed a wide range of music. In grade school he even played guitar at his church on Sundays—which I thought was odd, given his partying lifestyle. (It turns out that his love for music was pivotal in saving his life.) Bill knew from listening to THE WAVE that I loved Christian music. He also knew that Bob Dylan produced three albums that he thought I'd be interested in: Saved, Shot of Love and Slow Train Coming, all CCM Classics. So he invited me to his house, we hung out, listened to these albums, and from there our friendship developed.

Four friends. Four different walks of life. Yet each person fulfilled a different purpose for me, and all four demonstrated an unconditional commitment to helping me navigate my obstacles.

The obstacles along the way didn't redefine me, but they did redirect me. So often in our minds we make obstacles permanent in their existence, which causes us to stop. As I was redirected to R.T., Jan, Jim and Bill, we helped each other move forward in life.

In May, 1982, I accomplished my goal of graduating from high school the same year as my class. The irony of accomplishing this goal was its location: Humphrey Gymnasium, the place I dreamed about playing basketball in for Marquette High School. Humphrey Gymnasium no longer served as a reminder for what I didn't get to accomplish on the court; it served as the place where I would get a standing ovation—not for making a basket or getting a steal, but for beating the odds, overcoming obstacles and finishing the course...graduating.

I was in line with Jim, waiting to receive my diploma. The school principal, Larry Siewart, called my name—"David Alexander Cooks"—and with that, Jim pushed me up the ramp and onto the stage. I was greeted with a standing ovation by my peers—the same reception they gave me in January of 1980. I don't know who was smiling more at that moment, Jim or me. Rev. Bill Doran, S.J., the school's president, gave me my diploma. I shook Rev. Doran's hand, gave him a Susan B. Anthony dollar, and left the stage like all my fellow graduates did.

My high school career had ended, but there were a few things I needed to take care of before heading to my next stop: the University of Wisconsin-Whitewater.

I *still* missed basketball.

Chapter 5: Preparation

A Summer of Transition

There is nothing wrong with small beginnings.
Nothing is insignificant; Everything matters.

IT SOUNDS CLICHÉ, BUT FAITH, FAMILY, AND friends helped me complete high school and prepare for college. My dreams were still intact, as the nightmare of my spinal aneurysm could not kill them. The wheelchair couldn't kill them either. Only I could do that, and that wasn't an option. I was driven to be successful, and I was driven by the fear of being poor—I saw enough of that growing up.

I always wanted to be a businessman, specifically a banker, even though I wasn't really sure what that meant. I knew they wore suits to work, something otherwise reserved for Sundays, weddings or funerals where I grew up. I also knew that money had something to do with business, and that banks had a lot of money. So in my mind, becoming a banker would be the route I hoped to take.

Prior to freshman year of high school—well before the aneurysm—I applied for and was accepted into the INROADS pre-college program. INROADS is a national, non-profit organization dedicated to developing and placing talented underserved youth in local business and industry and preparing them for corporate and community leadership through workshops, mentoring and internships.

Debra Kenner, Director of INROADS Milwaukee, as well as the rest of the INROADS staff, modeled and reiterated that the importance of academic performance and rigor—even in high school—was necessary for achieving my business dreams. Going into high school, I was told the next four years would influence the next 40 years.

I heeded their advice, and by my junior year in high school, I was fortunate enough to serve as a student representative on the Milwaukee INROADS Advisory Board of Directors. It was in that capacity that I was introduced to some of the most influential business leaders in Milwaukee, including Fred Stratton, former CEO of Briggs and Stratton, and Jim Wigdale, former CEO of Marshall & Ilsley Bank. Both played important roles in my life as a Marquette High student and a business professional. My experience with INROADS gave me a great opportunity to learn from some of the brightest and most powerful people in business. More importantly, it was an affiliation that bolstered my self-esteem and confidence.

Fred Stratton took an interest in me both professionally and personally. He took the time to mentor me on the basics of business and the importance of networking. I later found out that he was responsible for securing financial assistance for my family in the form of an academic scholarship when I was in high school. This helped ease the financial burden that my family was under as a result of the additional medical bills caused by the aneurysm.

Additionally, it was Fred's advising and close relationship with Jim Wigdale that I believe led to my first job in banking during my junior year—a lockbox clerk at the M&I Data Center. I was excited about working again.

My first job growing up was delivering newspapers with my brother. We had two routes: one that covered the apartment complexes just north of Teutonia and Villard Avenues, and the other in the neighborhood projects and houses on 23rd and 24th Streets. The best part about delivering papers was when the Milwaukee Journal Sentinel's annual Christmas calendar came out. That's when we made the most money. People were very generous.

The part I liked the least—but probably benefited from the most—was delivering the Sunday newspaper. My brother and I would arrive at the "paper shack" around 4am to assemble the newspapers, pack them in the family station wagon (thanks, Dad, for getting up so early on the weekend to do the driving) and deliver them to the doorsteps. Rain or shine, hot or cold, sick or well, the papers had to be delivered on time and in good condition—every time.

For as long as I can remember, my parents ingrained in me to do my very best—no matter how large or small the task—or don't bother doing it at all. That advice and mindset came in handy when we were delivering papers, and it was even more applicable once I started at the M&I Data Center.

A lockbox clerk was not a glamorous position, but it represented a new beginning for me. It was another important step and opportunity as I continued the process of starting my life over. My job was processing insurance premium payments on an IBM 3762 machine for hours at a time, followed by filing the checks alphabetically and numerically. What others may have considered boring and mundane work, I saw as my path into banking.

Several key people at the M&I Data Center supported me. Richard Phalen, the manager overseeing all of the lockbox operations, made sure I had every opportunity to flourish in spite of my physical limitations and lack of business experience. He helped me understand the significance of the work I was doing and how it impacted the corporation's bottom line. Richard instilled confidence in me and positioned me for success; two keys of an effective leader and coach.

Linda Atwell sat across from me as I worked on the IBM 3762. She was easy to talk to, a pleasure to be around and made me feel comfortable; she treated me like I was another full-time employee, not a part-time high school worker. From the first day I met her, the wheelchair was never an issue for her.

Through our many conversations, it didn't take long for trust to build between us. That trust led to Linda becoming one of the first people outside of my family and high school friends with whom I openly discussed what it was like to be in a wheelchair. It was my opportunity to make someone else comfortable with me and break down another barrier. Linda and I became good friends.

As much as I appreciated the lockbox job, my goal was to make it to the M&I Bank headquarters in downtown Milwaukee, where Jim Wigdale worked. I wanted to wear three-button suits like he did. To have lunch with clients on the sixth floor in the executive dining room. To be where the action was. In the meantime, I made sure I met the quotas for the number of batches completed each day and got checks filed efficiently and accurately.

My hard work and attention to detail did not go unnoticed. In the spring of my senior year, I was awarded a four-year summer internship at the bank's headquarters. My confidence was at an all-time high. My plan to become a banker was on track. I was heading downtown.

The internship, part of the INROADS program, was designed to give me exposure to various departments throughout the bank and to show me how they worked together. The first summer at the bank, the months between finishing high school and beginning college, began with me counting currency in the bank vault. It wasn't the promotion I had expected. Who could see three-button suits in the vault?

Thankfully, I was good at counting and didn't have to stay in the vault for long. Next stop: the collections department. Collections was not an easy job. It took a while for me to discern between lies and truths as I attempted to collect payments from past due customers. Collections also taught me about compassion for those who were really struggling with job loss, sickness and compounding bills.

My final stop that summer was on the first floor of the bank working with Tom Deisinger, a retail personal banker. The first thing I noticed about Tom was his suits. He was a sharp dresser. A style guy. I liked that. He was also the consummate salesman with extraordinary interpersonal skills; he was patient, kind and a perfect mentor for me.

As the end of summer approached, I had to consider the next step: going to college. Independence.

I had completed high school and the summer internship at the bank, but there was one more test I needed to pass before I could head off to college: I needed to get my driver's license. Care Cab continued to ensure I made it to work on time during those summer months, but I was itching to get my license.

My driver's education wasn't like most of my peers. Instead of gas and brake pedals, I was introduced to hand controls and the spinner knob. The hand controls operated similar to a motorcycle: twist to accelerate, push in to brake. The spinner knob, located at two o'clock on the steering wheel, assisted with making turns.

The first time out, my instructor took me into downtown Milwaukee. While driving across the Wisconsin Avenue Bridge, I turned the wheel a little too much, lost my balance and thought for sure I would run into another car. Thankfully, my instructor had a brake on his side of the car and deployed it just in time.

My instructor never flinched. Right after that, he instructed me to drive onto the busy interstate.

"What?" I asked. "Are you kidding me?" I couldn't believe we were doing that after what had just happened.

He looked at me, shrugged, and said, "Hey, you're learning how to drive."

His words did nothing to slow down my fast heartbeat. I was scared—for both of us. Sometimes you have to do the scary thing and trust people who have been there before.

But it didn't take long for me to adjust to the sensitivity of the controls. The ride on the interstate went a lot better with not as much turning involved. I was pretty confident that I could do this and eventually not have to rely on Care Cab.

From there, I had three more "hands-on" lessons. Parallel parking was a challenge, but no more near accidents occurred. Independence was within my grasp—literally. I passed the written exam and the behind-the-wheel test on my first try. I was awarded my driver's license in time for me to go to college.

PREPARATION

The summer before college, I was able to get a car—a sky-blue, 1980 Oldsmobile Omega coupe, fully loaded with power windows, power locks and an aftermarket Alpine stereo system that included a CD player and a cassette player.

My summer was now complete. I earned my diploma, worked at the bank and received my driver's license. I would no longer have to rely on Care Cab for my transportation. Life was good. I was about to head into the unknown world of college life—but like most 18-year-olds, I was ready.

Chapter 6: Plan

The College Experience: Radio

Be intentional about making other people's lives better.
Do it on purpose, for purpose.

My decision to attend the University of Wisconsin–Whitewater was an easy one once I visited the school in the summer of 1981 with my father. It was a good choice professionally, as the stellar reputation of the Carlson College of Business would help me get closer to wearing suits downtown with financial VIPs. It was a good choice physically because of the school's commitment to accessibility for students with physical challenges and its work with diverse students. There would be no more loading docks and cumbersome elevators just to get to my first class of the day.

The final selling point for me was its proximity. UW-Whitewater was a goldilocks 45 minutes from home. It was close enough to return if my family or I needed something, yet far enough away for me to have the "college experience" I desired. Like many college grads, those years helped me to find my way, understand my natural gifts and express my core passions.

Going away for college was part of the process in our family. My brother, a junior at the University of Wisconsin–Eau Claire, set the precedent for us when he moved out a few years earlier. I had been in a wheelchair for almost three years, and although I had never spent a night away from home, I was confident in my ability to be self-sufficient—especially at a school set up for it.

Driving myself to Whitewater on move-in day was the ultimate act of independence for me. With my parents following behind, I made it safely to the school, and they helped me unpack and ready my new home: a dorm on the sixth floor of the west tower of Wells Hall.

Two things stood out on campus immediately: girls and wheelchairs. They were all over the place. There were no other students in wheelchairs at my all-boys high school, my job or my church. I had grown accustomed to the double takes that came with being the only one. That wasn't the case anymore. At UW–Whitewater, I would have the opportunity to socialize with and to get to know others in wheelchairs.

But as strange as it sounds, I was initially a little uncomfortable around other people with physical challenges and wheelchair users. Unlike my family and friends, I didn't benefit from the experiences of interacting with people "like me." I found I was guilty of dealing the same things I had learned to "deal with"—staring, double takes and prejudging. Until then, it hadn't been a two-way street for me.

I didn't date much in high school after the aneurysm. It wasn't that I didn't have the skills, but my confidence had been shaken when the girl I was seeing unceremoniously dumped me because "you're in a wheelchair."

That hurt.

After that, I wondered if I'd ever find a girl who would like me despite the fact I was in a wheelchair. Those thoughts also moved into Wells Hall with me at UW-Whitewater. But so did a lot of attractive girls. While it's true that how you leave one place is how you enter the next one, after looking around in this new place, it didn't take much to convince myself that it was time to get back into the game.

Classes didn't start for a few days, which gave me ample opportunities to get to know the campus and make a new group of friends—and maybe even a girlfriend. There were parties everywhere—and I mean everywhere. I made the rounds and wound up meeting people who shared my perspective on drinking and drugs: It wasn't part of our family histories, and it wasn't the least bit tempting for us to partake in. I avoided drugs on the Milwaukee playgrounds, which were in abundant supply. I avoided them in high school, and I wanted to keep my streak alive in college, too.

The fact that I found others—including girls—on campus who didn't need to drink, do drugs or experiment with some combination of the two just to have fun was comforting. It was a relief knowing I wasn't the only one.

I dated several girls in college, but the wheelchair always became a sticking point once the prospect of sharing a long-term relationship arose. Slowly, I came to terms with this. I couldn't take it personally. Of all people, I understood the challenges that came along with being with someone in a wheelchair. And at that age, I couldn't blame someone for hesitating.

Despite not finding my soul mate in college, the relationships I did have helped me grow immensely. They gave me the experience necessary to process what I wanted (and didn't want) in a woman. I was heartened that there were girls out there who still found me interesting—and good-looking. There was more to me than the wheelchair, and I was confident that I wouldn't have to compromise my values to find someone who loved me and would commit to me unconditionally.

There were plenty of times during that first week of college and throughout my four years at UW-Whitewater when I had the opportunity to compromise. It's often easier and more comfortable to settle than to stand firm, especially alone. However, if there was one thing I understood about compromise—whether it dealt with work, school, girls, parties or anything else—it was that it led to more compromise.

I didn't always get it right, but I got better and better at turning grey areas, which contained consequences that could move me away from my goals, into black-and-white ones. And as soon as they became black and white, I drew the line and refused to compromise.

I couldn't predict every situation I would have to face in college, but I kept some non-negotiables in my back pocket. For those, I knew my boundaries and planned escape routes if the circumstances warranted it.

Between the wheelchairs, girls, parties, having my own space, and sharing meals with floor mates (that were as much of social events as food events), college represented another new beginning—another change of clothes for me. Speaking of which, getting undressed in room 668 of Wells Hall was different from getting undressed at home or at Sacred Heart. No nurses or family to help me. I was on my own and had to make it work.

One of my top priorities was to visit WSUW 91.7 FM, the university radio station. I loved my experience DJ-ing on THE WAVE in high school, and my goal was to join the WSUW staff and host my own show someday.

On the day before classes officially began, I headed to Hyer Hall to see if I could meet with Steve Shields, the radio's program director. I knew Hyer Hall was on the other end of campus, but I didn't anticipate the workout I would get on my way there. A couple of hills with a steady (but not too steep) grade made blocks feel like miles. It reminded me that I wasn't in the best physical shape anymore.

Tired but excited, I took the elevator up to the radio station and knocked on Mr. Shields' door. He welcomed me into his office, and not long after our greeting, he looked at me sideways.

"Has anyone ever told you that you have a very unique voice?" Mr. Shields asked. "You know, a little James Earl Jones-like?"

"As in *This is CNN...*" I said, impersonating the legend.

"Yes!" he said laughing. "That James Earl Jones."

The conversation quickly turned back to business.

"So what do you see yourself doing here? Jazz? R&B? Pop?"

"Well, I was thinking more along the lines of a specialty show. A Christian music show."

Mr. Shields paused. "We don't have one of those, and I'm not sure how that would work, given we're at a state school. In fact, I don't think we've ever had one."

He didn't say no, I thought. He only said they didn't have one, not that they couldn't have one.

"What did you have in mind?" Mr. Shields continued.

"It's kind of like what I did in high school," I said. "I was thinking of putting together a show that included all music genres, but with Christian lyrics. Christian rock, rap, gospel, urban, country and traditional—all in one."

"Hmm, it's a unique concept. And we do have Sunday morning slots open, which I've had trouble filling for years. I'll need to think about it, check on if we can even do something like that, and get back to you. I hope you understand."

"Absolutely, I do. I'm excited to get started."

"Before we go, I have a couple more questions for you. Even if we could do a Christian-themed show, we don't have any albums in the studio. How do you plan on getting the music for your show?"

"I have a milk crate with about 40 albums that I brought from home," I replied. "I could use them to get the show started, but I'm not sure how to get additional music for the show. Would you recommend that I contact the companies listed on the albums and request that they add us to their list of radio stations that receive products?"

"Yes," Mr. Shields said. "We don't have established relationships with those companies, so it would be up to you to make that happen."

"Done," I said.

"Secondly, how will you get around campus? Do you have transportation? You'd be the first DJ in a wheelchair we've ever had here, and I want to make sure it will work for both of us if we decide to move forward."

"I have a car here on campus. No worries there."

"Excellent," he said. "I'll check on it then—but in the meantime, I'll have you meet Frankie K. who hosts our jazz show. He can show you the ropes once you get settled here."

I thanked Mr. Shields and left his office feeling pretty pumped up. I was really confident that I would be getting the chance to be on the radio.

On my way back to my dorm, I stopped in the Roseman Building across from the Student Union. Disabled student services offices were located there. I signed up for an informational meeting to be held later that week and proceeded to give myself a tour of the rest of the building.

There were lots of classrooms with little desks that seemed to suit an elementary school more than a college. At the end of the hall was the physical therapy room, fully equipped with mats, parallel bars and a universal weight set, and nudged in the corner was a bunch of extra wheelchairs. As I peered into the room, I heard a familiar, uneven, echoing thud coming from around the corridor. I followed it instinctively; I had a feeling I knew the origin of the sounds. The echoes grew louder, and I could smell the strange mixture of sweat and hardwood floor that confirmed my intuition that a pick-up basketball game was underway.

The gym was around the corner from the physical therapy room. I opened the door and went in, expecting to see a regular basketball game; instead, for the first time I saw wheelchair basketball being played. Those extra wheelchairs in the PT room must have been sports chairs for people to use. I quickly observed that sports chairs had no brakes, no tip bars and cambered wheels, which made them noticeably faster than everyday wheelchairs. It was a different game than regular basketball, but it had the same level of intensity and physicality.

Within the first few minutes of me watching, one of the players got knocked out of his wheelchair. Instead of the game stopping, he popped right back into his chair and continued playing.

I had never seen anything like it. It looked fun—and intense—especially for someone who could barely make it from one side of campus to the other without getting winded. But it triggered memories of playing on the playground, playing after school, playing the game I fell in love with at a young age. It reminded me how much I missed it, and I could feel my passion rekindling now that I had witnessed an avenue for pursuing it.

I left the gym without speaking to anyone.

After the first week of classes, I still hadn't heard back from Steve Shields at the radio station—so I decided to stop by and see what was going on myself. Nothing yet. No decision. However, in the interim, Mr. Shields arranged for me to co-host a show called "Directions in Jazz" with its host, Frankie K. It was a "tryout," I thought, just like in basketball. I was excited and ready for my audition.

Frankie K was a jazz guy through and through: He was smooth and mellow, and the words that passed his lips were like poetry. I loved working with him on-air that night in the studio. The featured jazz artist for that show was world-renowned guitarist George Benson, and we played many of his notable hits—including "Breezin," "On Broadway," "Give Me the Night," and, of course, "This Masquerade."

Frankie showed me how to work the board, how to get the weather reports, and how to perfect the art of speaking over a song intro. It was a bit different from spinning records in the Blue and Gold Room at Marquette High. But Frankie K thought I was a natural and that I had a voice perfect for smooth jazz and late-night radio. They were flattering comments, but I was still banking on having my own show.

A few days later, Mr. Shields granted that wish.

He liked what he heard when I teamed with Frankie K, and he offered me an 8:00 a.m. until noon Sunday slot, where I could feature Christian music exclusively. As I processed the offer, I marveled at how the situation ascended from nothing, with everything in doubt, to four whole hours—double the time they allotted to other specialty shows.

I left his office on an all-time high. I was going to be on the radio! I didn't waste any time contacting record companies across the United States, asking to be added to their mailing lists for promotional albums, singles, and eventually CDs.

Timing is always one of the keys to success. And fortunately for me, CCM was attracting new audiences every day. It was experiencing exponential growth right when I got my foot in the door of the industry, so I had no problem getting my hands on new, free products during that time. I wouldn't have to rely solely on my milk crate collection for long.

I decided to call the show "Morning Inspiration," and it debuted on Sunday, September 12, 1982. It was the best mix of Christian music in Southeastern Wisconsin. The first song I played was Amy Grant's number one hit song, "Sing Your Praise to the Lord." And as they say, the rest was history.

Every Saturday before a show, I would pick the songs and order them—ensuring a healthy mix of styles and genres, with an urban contemporary or gospel song intentionally placed in every third slot.

Every Sunday, I was up at 6 a.m. in order to get to the studio and finish prepping before airtime. Getting up that early on a Sunday may be a big deal to most college students, but the 4 a.m. paper routes I had in high school made 6 a.m. feel like nothing. Instead of delivering newspapers, I now delivered music that my community needed—rain, shine, sleet or snow.

Once my mic was hot, my goal was to bring together people from all walks of life through the power and majesty of Christian music. In doing so, I strived to find my own way of positively impacting the Whitewater campus and community. And it did—for both close friends and complete strangers.

Bill Thompson, one of my best friends in high school, attended the University of Wisconsin-Madison. It was about a 45-minute drive from Madison to Whitewater, and Bill didn't have any form of transportation. Still, at least twice each semester—especially during our junior and senior years—Bill would hitchhike his way to Whitewater's campus and spend the weekend with me. I wasn't thrilled about his mode of transportation, but my offers to give him a ride were rejected time and time again.

Bill was going through a rough patch in his life. The drinking, the drugs and the partying he indulged in (and what made him popular in high school) had taken their toll on him. He realized that he needed to undergo a lifestyle transition—a wardrobe change—not only to save his grades, but his life. Just like it did in high school, music became the point of connection between us.

When Bill visited, we spent most of our nights chatting, hanging out and listening to his favorite group—the Winans—and he wouldn't leave on Sunday until after the radio show finished. The music of "Morning Inspiration" had become an outlet he used to heal and turn his life around. He eventually stopped drinking and doing drugs, opting instead for a healthier means of entertainment. But the show's impact had been far reaching on campus even before Bill began his regular commute to Whitewater.

One night during the spring semester of my freshman year, a stranger—a redheaded student—knocked on my door and asked if she could talk to me. She told me she liked my radio show, and as far as I was concerned that was enough of a reason to start a conversation.

"I'm pregnant," she said. "And I don't know what to do."

My eyes widened. I couldn't believe she was telling me something so deeply personal—and to a freshman she heard on the radio of all people. It was the first time I realized how big the show was becoming and how it was impacting its listeners.

She told me she was thinking about aborting the child. She was frightened at the prospect and responsibility of having and raising a child on her own, and she was terrified of what her family and friends would say. It was a new and bizarre experience for me, too, but I listened, I empathized, and I impressed upon her that although it wouldn't be easy, I thought she should have the child—and that she wasn't alone in dealing with her circumstances. Countless women had been in her position and came out as winners.

I told her my belief that if it's in your life, you are equipped to handle and overcome it. Instead of asking, "Why me?" ask, "Why not me?"

It's amazing what the human will is capable of dealing with. After all, our ability to endure is always greater than our willingness to endure. It's a shift in the narrative, but a necessary one when overcoming obstacles.

She thanked me for listening to her, for my advice and for not condemning her. She left without giving me any indication of what she was thinking, and I thought I would probably not see her again.

During my junior year, I met a freshman named Bill Anciaux. Despite a confidence that teetered on being arrogant and turned some people off, Bill and I formed an instant connection. As far as I was concerned, he had a right to be confident. Bill had the most remarkable voice I'd ever heard. He sounded exactly like a disc jockey should sound—from his pitch, to his tone, to his pace, to his timbre. He had it all. Once he arrived, the Golden Throat awards I had received the first two years fell into Bill's hands.

Bill mentored and challenged me to become better on the air, and he said I mentored and challenged him to become better off the air. Together we made some great promos for the radio station, including one for "Morning Inspiration" that I think was our best collaboration. The commercial featured both our voices with "Cover Me," a track from Michael James Murphy as the backdrop.

Our friendship grew over the next couple of years and centered around music and faith. Bill had lots of questions in both areas, and I tried to provide him with answers—first with my life and second with my words. As Bill discovered the answers to his questions, he became more immersed in the music. A natural succession for "Morning Inspiration" was in place.

What started as a dream and a milk crate full of Christian albums ended with over 2000 LPs, 1500 CDs, 115 shows, 460 hours of programming, 5730 songs played, and hundreds of music and concert ticket giveaways. "Morning Inspiration" went on to become one of the station's flagship specialty shows, which blossomed more and more each year. It gained greater prominence than I ever imagined, and I didn't want the show to leave with me when I graduated.

After I graduated in May of 1986, Bill Anciaux became the new voice of "Morning Inspiration" and made it his own. He renamed the show "Power Source," and he kept the voice of Christian music alive on WSUW 91.7 FM.

The gimmicks I used to increase listener interaction (merchandise giveaways, concert tickets, etc.) made things exciting—but the feeling of having a positive impact on the Whitewater community was what made it a powerful and lasting experience in my mind. People's lives changed—including mine—all because of some Sunday morning inspiration.

A few years later, I visited a church on Milwaukee's East Side for Sunday morning service. A young woman approached me afterward. She was holding a small child with a cleft lower lip and a deformed hand, and she asked if I remembered her. I didn't, but before I could say anything else, she fell into a flurry of thank-you's for persuading her to give birth to the "light of her life."

She had named him David.

"Morning Inspiration" didn't just change lives; it saved at least one.

Chapter 7: Possibilities

The College Experience:
Wheelchair Basketball

*Making adjustments on and off the court, and in life,
are pivotal to success. Be willing to do things differently.*

AFTER FINDING "MORNING INSPIRATION" TO fulfill one of my passions, I thought it was time to follow another. Ever since I stumbled upon that group of guys playing wheelchair basketball at the Roseman Building, a tiny, curious tug inside me wondered if I could orchestrate the game seated as well as I did on my feet.

Every day in my dorm, I received a daily visual reminder—and sometimes a verbal one—of wheelchair basketball. Guy Perry, one of the guys I saw playing that day, lived on my floor at Wells Hall and encouraged me to give the sport a try from the moment we met. Like me, he had a car, attended the Carlson College of Business and valued self-sufficiency. In a lot of ways, he reminded me of Tony Otters from the rehabilitation center—who was at that point a senior at the University of Wisconsin–Whitewater, well on his way to his dream of becoming a physician.

Guy Perry had suffered a spinal cord injury from an accidental gunshot wound at the age of 12. Still, he had an infectious love for life and never complained about anything. He tried to do everything with no limitations.

But even with Guy's best encouragement, I wasn't quite ready to give wheelchair basketball a try. My excuse was that I wanted to get a good start academically, but in reality, fear held me back.

Guy was persistent. He encouraged me to get involved in as many things on campus as possible as a great way to make friends, build relationships and enjoy the college experience. He saw something in me. And if he couldn't convince me himself, he wanted to let someone else try. He had someone in mind that he wanted to introduce me to. Since this other guy, Ricky Chones, was an avid fisherman like me, I made it a priority to meet him.

Ricky was another person I saw playing that pick-up game of wheelchair basketball. Despite being born as a double amputee, basketball was in his blood—literally and figuratively. Ricky was from Racine, Wisconsin and was related to Jim Chones—one of the greatest basketball players to ever come from the state of Wisconsin.

Ricky was a "stat sheet stuffer." He could do it all on the hardwood—shoot, dribble, and rebound. On the court, he was all business and the most competitive person I've ever met. He didn't just want to win; he wanted to destroy his opponents—even in pick-up games—and required his teammates to produce, or they'd hear about it from him. Off the court, he was a totally different person. He loved life and telling hilarious stories and jokes, and one couldn't mistake his distinct, infectious, trademark laugh. We spent a lot of time on the fishing bank, talking hoops.

Guy, Ricky, and head coach Frank Burns (who was one of the most respected coaches in the game at that time) were persistent—

but not pushy—in their efforts to persuade me to play. I reminisced about my playing days, remembering the competition and camaraderie that I hadn't yet found a sufficient replacement for in my life. In the end, I decided it was too good of an opportunity for me to pass up.

I instantly regretted signing up to play, because preseason conditioning was insane. Wind sprints, hills and dips filled my days when I wasn't in class, studying or working on "Morning Inspiration." Dips were by far the most physically demanding thing I had to do. The physical therapy room contained a set of parallel bars for us do them. I'd have to roll up to the parallel bars and lift my legs up onto a strap that connected tightly on both bars. From there, I'd grab the bars and hoist myself out of the chair, legs straight out in front of me. One of my teammates would remove the wheelchair from under me, and I'd have to lift my body up and let gravity drop me back down—and repeat until my arms quivered precariously.

And that was just the first set.

In the first days of preseason conditioning, I could only do a few. But by increasing the amount I did every few weeks, I was up to 25 dips by senior year.

In-season practices weren't much easier than preseason conditioning. It was pretty much non-stop pushing for two hours, and as sore as my arms and shoulders were, my hands bore the brunt of it: nicks, cuts, skin tears and jammed fingers scarred my hands until they formed deep callouses—the sign of a veteran baller. There was eventually no more sting when I soaked my hands in alcohol.

Wheelchair basketball was neither for the faint of heart nor the mentally weak. The first time I was knocked out of my wheelchair, I thought for sure that practice would stop as I struggled my way back to the chair. Wrong. Practice—much like life—kept on going, even when I fell. It was up to me to get back in the game.

Getting knocked out of my chair was pretty much a rite of passage. It happened early and often, until I learned how to properly maneuver a sports wheelchair and how to absorb contact so it wouldn't take me all the way to the floor.

"Welcome to wheelchair college basketball, Rook!"

Not Gus Williams, not Cooks, but "Rook." I guess it was a term of endearment. Guy and Chones made sure I knew I was the new kid on the block, but it wouldn't take long for me to earn their respect as a player.

The first day of practice, Coach Burns put the ball in my hands and told me to run the team. The point guard is the coach on the floor. An extension of the head coach. The floor leader. It was the same position I played when I was walking, and it came with the same responsibilities. I had to know when to be aggressive, when to slow down the pace, and how to effectively communicate the plays and the coach's directives to the team. I reveled not only in having the ball in my hands with a game in the balance, but in being the leader—the person on the court responsible for guiding the ship.

But playing point guard on a wheelchair basketball team was different from playing on a traditional one. Threading the needle and dropping no-look bounce passes were difficult to do in a wheelchair, and often less effective. I also needed to be extra conscious of who was on the receiving end of my passes.

POSSIBILITIES

No two disabilities are alike. Balance, hand usage and arm strength are directly related to the type of disability a player has. If a player has trouble catching the ball because of a disability with his hands, that player's role will likely be to set screens to get shooters open. As the floor leader, it was my responsibility to get the ball to the right players where they could be successful. Quickly processing and knowing who else was on the court was a prerequisite for playing point guard and was essential to our team's success.

My first collegiate game was at the UNI-Dome at the University of Northern Iowa. This was also my first time ever being away from home. We arrived at our hotel in Cedar Falls, only to discover that the room I was to share with Ricky wasn't wheelchair accessible—narrow doorways, furniture that made it difficult to get around, and the worst: no bathroom access. We went back downstairs to the lobby to request another room, but there weren't any other vacancies in the hotel.

Man, what we gonna do?

I started panicking, but Ricky started laughing—which didn't curtail my anxiety much.

"Relax, Rook; it's gonna be fine," he said. "Let's just see if we can get a couple extra chairs from the team's other rooms. We're going to build a bridge."

Build a bridge? I thought. With chairs? He must have left his mind at the Wisconsin-Iowa border.

Following his direction, Ricky and I rounded up as many chairs as we could and he began lining them up next to each other, leading right into our bathroom and next to the toilet. It was brilliant. I never would have thought of that.

When my wheelchair wouldn't fit through the hotel bathroom, I only saw a problem—not a solution. I had temporarily stopped, remaining steadfast in my problem instead of devising out-of-the-box solutions. I was a "rook" in more ways than one. I quickly learned to lean on my teammates on and off the court, as many of them had a lot more experience with life in a wheelchair than I did.

My first road trip was a success. We won our games, I scored my first collegiate points, and I was part of building a bridge.

For the next four years, I was fortunate enough to play with some really talented players: Guy Perry, Ricky Chones, Ben Hunter and Elmer Megna, just to name a few. During my senior year, we made it to the National Championship game against the University of Illinois. It was a classic championship game: lots of lead changes and great players making great plays in the big moments.

In the waning moments of the game, with our team down two points, I was fouled on a drive to the basket. I wasn't in the act of shooting, but we were in the bonus—so I had 1-and-1 free throw attempts.

I positioned my wheelchair at the free throw line, bounced the ball a couple of times, and calmly sank the first free throw. The referee passed me the ball again, and I repeated my routine: two dribbles and a shot. It felt good off the fingertips, creating the necessary backspin that often coaxed the ball through the net. But it rimmed out. No overtime. No redo. We lost.

Earning second team All-Tournament was an honor, but it didn't take away much of the sting. The loss still haunts me to this day, but it wasn't about me. It was about our team, who fought so hard to get there. And to have the ball in my hands with the game on the line and a chance to put our team into overtime—it doesn't get much better than that. The fact I had that opportunity was a winning situation in and of itself.

It wasn't the way I wanted my wheelchair basketball career to end, but that's the nature of championship games: there's only one champion. Still, that disappointment did not define my career. I hadn't been able to make the state championship basketball team at Marquette High School, so being part of the UW-Whitewater Rolling Warhawks basketball program's run filled the void left by the aneurysm.

Between working towards my degree, the radio show and wheelchair basketball, my four years at UW-Whitewater flew by. Before I knew it, graduation was around the corner—with my love for the game of basketball alive and well. I was looking forward to moving on—to building a bridge to the next stage of my life, a career as a banker at M&I Bank. But my involvement with basketball was just beginning. My zeal for the game was still there, and I was ready to find out-of-the-box ways to enhance/feed/fulfill this passion.

Obstacles don't define you; they redirect you.

Chapter 8: Partnership

Banking and Basketball

In life, like in basketball, you're judged by how well you can get the job done. Performance, whether good or bad, answers questions.

WHILE WORKING TOWARD MY BACHELOR'S degree in finance, I spent my summers interning with M&I Bank. Rotating from department to department those four summers, I was able to discern what I liked and disliked within the banking sector.

During my final summer, I got a taste of what commercial lending was all about. Commercial lenders analyzed the financial strength of businesses seeking to borrow money and then determined whether to move forward—and if so, at what cost. And then there was the relationship (PR) side of the job: the meetings, the lunches, the facility tours, the sporting events. I loved every part of it, including the three-button suits. Commercial lending was where all the action was; it was where I wanted to be.

At the end of that summer, M&I Bank offered me a full-time job as a commercial loan trainee. I accepted.

To this day, that was by far the best corporate job I've ever had. Commercial lending had the perfect blend of customer entertainment, financial analysis, business development, critical thinking and business presentations that suited my skill set. I was surrounded by really bright, really nice, and really fun people. I didn't mind the ten-hour days when I got to spend them with people like that.

We were truly a team—a team composed of veterans and rookies, specialists and jacks-of-all-trades—but still one team. What made it such a positive experience was the veterans' willingness to share their knowledge with everyone. They weren't intimidated by the influx of young, hungry talent. They understood that helping us made themselves, the company and the team better.

Peter Van Housen and Harry J. Metrusias, two seasoned lending officers who specialized in healthcare and large manufacturing companies, took me under their wings and showed me how to play the commercial lending game. They helped minimize one of my biggest challenges—accessibility in the marketplace—as they coached me and put me in positions in which I could succeed.

Chemistry and culture are just as important as talent in the success of a business or a sports team. M&I Bank had both, and we were a close-knit team. Where else could you work and have lunch in the cafeteria at a table across from Jack Puelicher, the bank's CEO, or regularly ride the elevator with him—cigar and all? Every holiday season, the bank gave each employee a box of fruit. It felt like a family.

My primary professional goal was to become a commercial loan officer for the bank. The process of going from a trainee to an associate to an officer took approximately five years. My secondary goal was to obtain my MBA. The five-year work plan aligned perfectly with the window I gave myself to assess my professional progress to determine what my next move would be. I was well on my way toward accomplishing my goals, until I suffered a setback.

One of the negative side effects of experiencing an aneurysm at such a young age was that as I grew as a teenager, I did so without the abdominal and lower back muscles essential to support my spine. Concurrently, I developed a severe case of scoliosis. Doctors were concerned about long-term internal ramifications—especially on my heart—and they recommended surgery.

Surgery? I thought. Again? Man, I thought I'd be walking by now—not having more surgery.

Nonetheless, the decision to go ahead with the surgery wasn't a difficult one. Cosmetically, it was appealing; and from a long-term health perspective, it was a no-brainer.

It had been eight years since I had been a patient at St. Michael's Hospital, but I was back again. However, the uncertainty around my diagnosis then was replaced with certainty this time around. Still, as with any kind of surgery, there is risk—especially when it involved screws, Harrington rods and spinal fusion.

The surgery succeeded in stabilizing my spine and correcting the curvature, but a few days later, I contracted a staph infection in the area of the incision. It wound up being just the beginning of a grueling 12-month recovery.

There was the two months of intravenous antibiotics. There was the back brace, which further limited my mobility and impacted my independence—something I took immense pride in maintaining. Then, there was the pain. The Harrington rods triggered inconsistent jolts from the sharp twinges of pain between my shoulder blades.

Would this be my new normal? Would being in a wheelchair actually prevent me from accomplishing my goals?

Lots of questions—even a few doubts—crept into my mind. I was concerned about my job and whether I'd be able to meet the requirements with my mobility so hampered. I hadn't planned on something new to have to deal with and overcome. I had grown weary of the fight and just wanted a break.

For a time, I forgot my own formula: to take one day at a time, moment by moment. To win each moment so I would win each day. Looking beyond the day, beyond the moment, would only cause stress. I wasn't going to quit; I was just tired and needed a pep talk.

During this time, I had an opportunity at the bank to work with Sandy Cicero, a retail banker who had account responsibilities for the Milwaukee Bucks and many of its players. My love for the game had not diminished over the years, and working with Sandy on these accounts was just what I needed. We attended games, networked and interacted with the players and ownership. It was right in my wheelhouse.

Kathy Scott, a friend from my church, connected me with the Bucks even more. Kathy introduced me to players like Terry Cummings, Paul Pressey and Sidney Moncrief. In addition to our love for basketball, these players and I also shared a strong faith, which they each reflected in how they carried themselves on and off the court. It was faith—not basketball—that probably allowed us to relate to each other so easily.

We often met at Mr. Perkins Family Restaurant, an iconic soul food restaurant in the heart of Milwaukee, to share a meal and talk about life. My favorite meal there was chicken and dumplings. Their wall of fame was incredible: It contained Polaroid pictures of celebrities, politicians and athletes who had dined there, and for me to share a table and many meals and conversations with some of these individuals was an amazing experience.

Terry Cummings and I became good friends. He and his cousin, Percy Bady, had an entertainment company that specialized in writing, recording and producing Christian music with artists such as The Winans. Although I was a couple of years removed from "Morning Inspiration," I still listened and bought the music. Thanks to Terry, I now had another way of staying connected with one of my passions.

While playing for the Milwaukee Bucks, Terry hosted an annual charity all-star game called the VIC at the Mecca, the home court of the Bucks. He would get players from around the NBA to participate, and Terry, a Chicago native, had the pull to persuade athletes who lived or grew up in Chicago to participate in the game.

M&I Bank served as the primary sponsor for the VIC event, and I was designated as the bank representative responsible for ensuring that things ran smoothly. The best perk for me was gaining locker room access prior to and after the game. I was a kid in a candy store, interacting with some of the best players in the world in the sport I absolutely adored.

One of my other responsibilities was presenting the game's MVP with a check that he would donate to a charity. That year, Michael Jordan played and won MVP honors. For a few moments on a June summer day, I forgot about the pain and discomfort I was experiencing and relished in the moment as I sat between Terry Cummings and Michael Jordan, shaking hands and presenting the MVP award and check to arguably the greatest of all time. What an experience!

As that summer progressed, though, I could no longer ignore the pain and my reduced mobility. I had been in discussion with the surgeons for some time about my options, and the only one that made sense was to have the Harrington rods removed—even if it meant being left with a curvature in my spine.

But there was another tradeoff, too. I'd have to permanently give up playing wheelchair basketball with Ricky Chones and the Racine South Shore Breakers. I'd have to find another way to satisfy my basketball itch.

If I had to give up wheelchair basketball in exchange for being pain-free again, I had to do it. I looked forward to getting back to work and performing at the level I expected for myself. That wasn't happening over the past year.

Even though the surgery had a negative impact on my productivity and overall performance during my first 30 months with the bank, I was promoted from a commercial loan trainee to an associate. Despite the physical setback, I was still on track for meeting my goal of being an officer of the bank in five years. The promotion to associate came right on time, too—exactly when I needed a self-esteem boost.

With the promotion came increased responsibilities and expectations. It was time to generate some serious new business for the bank. Meeting the 30-calls-per-month quota was never a huge concern—lots of ways to make that happen—but closing the deals was always the challenge. I also had to be certain I found and made good deals for the bank. I would need some help with that. I needed a coach to show me the ropes.

That coach was Mark Hogan, a rising star at M&I Bank: a well-respected dealmaker pegged as a future business leader at the bank or elsewhere. And he loved basketball as much as I did. It was banking and basketball with us. We ate lunch with clients on the sixth floor, entertained them at Bucks games in the company suite, and made cold calls together and presented loans on Thursday mornings together. Mark wasn't the easiest coach to play for, so to speak, because he constantly pushed me to do more, pay attention to detail and be the best version of myself. But because of that—and like any great coach would do—he pulled things out of me that I didn't know I had. With Mark on my team, I was well on my way to becoming an officer.

Mark pushed me to take on positions of leadership outside of banking, too. He was the first person who suggested I give coaching basketball a try. I started coaching one of the bank teams, but my first real opportunity in coaching didn't come for a few more years. And like most opportunities, they happen when you least expect them to.

One of my favorite things to do during the long, sometimes grueling Wisconsin winters was to go back to my alma mater and watch the Marquette High School varsity basketball games. Memories would swirl through me the moment I entered the gymnasium, and I watched the games with the same intensity I remember playing them.

Little did I know that Marquette High's coach, Paul Noack, an inductee in the Wisconsin Coaches Hall of Fame, often referenced me during his pregame and halftime speeches to inspire his players to reach for a little extra and outwork the opponents. Word about these speeches spread, eventually to Tim Larkin, father to Kevin, who played on Marquette High's team and who went on to play for Old Dominion University.

Tim introduced himself to me at halftime during of one of the games, and after that we had several opportunities to talk during that season. After a few conversations, Tim and I realized how much we had in common. We loved talking ball, but we shared a zeal for life, too—and our conversations veered toward brainstorming ways of applying life situations into basketball. Our pre, during and postgame conversations grew into a mutual admiration and friendship.

Tim was one of the founders of The Vic Tanny Warriors, a summer AAU team that travelled across the country competing in tournaments. Because he thought I could have a positive impact on the players in a program that was already regarded highly for its talent and character, Tim offered me an assistant coaching position with the Warriors alongside head coach Ric Cobb and assistant coaches Will Allen and Bill Marifky.

I jumped at the opportunity, and I was willing to do anything they asked of me. As it turned out, my greatest asset was just being me: I used my personality to build relationships with the young athletes on the team.

It didn't take long for me to realize I had a knack for it. I was gifted to motivate and inspire the players to go beyond their limits, to push them past their comfort levels, and to always stay hungry— the same lessons Mark Hogan instilled in me in the business world. AAU was no joke—and life isn't, either. In life, like in basketball, you're judged by how well you can get the job done— and if you can't, they'll find someone who can.

And that summer, every player pushed me, too. Besides making me a better coach, every player volunteered to push me in my wheelchair and to talk with me—not because they were told to, but because they wanted to learn from me.

I impressed upon each one of them that even if they didn't think they could do something on the basketball court or in life, I knew they could. The moment they became satisfied was the moment someone was ready to supplant them, so they had to be aggressive and be driven by the next play. They couldn't be afraid of making mistakes.

Everyone—and I mean everyone—had something to offer the team and the world, if even just a handshake, a conversation, a smile or a little coaching about the full court press. The sooner they realized that, the sooner they could make themselves and the world better than the day before. It was in those moments that I began to realize how much of a positive impact I could have on those around me.

Coaching AAU, and coaching that group of guys in particular, was a privilege in every sense of the word. It brought me into contact with some of the best coaches and basketball programs in the country. I was just getting my feet wet with coaching, and now I wanted full immersion. I would be all-in. I don't like doing something 50% or 75% or 90%. If something was worthy of my time and energy, I would give it all my attention and effort.

It wasn't success that motivated me, but being significant inspired every word and action I took. I wanted people to respect me for who I was, not for what I'd done or because I was in a wheelchair. When you're a part of something where you feel like you're serving a purpose greater than yourself, that's the ultimate reward.

For the summers from 1989 to 1991, when I wasn't at work I was on the traveling circuit with the Vic Tanny Warriors. In addition to learning how to coach and inspire our players to be their best, I was busy networking. I was building relationships with college coaches from across the nation and leveraging those relationships and opportunities for the benefit of others for years to come. Jim Molinari, the head coach at Bradley University from 1991 to 2002, was the first coach at the collegiate level to invite me to work his summer camps. This served as a springboard to work other camps throughout the country during my weekends and time off, which expanded my coaching network. Molinari and his staff—Rob Judon and Ritchie McKay—were instrumental in creating opportunities for me for many years, including Division I assistant coaching positions.

Coaching basketball was taking on greater significance in my life, and I believe it was because the daily challenges of basketball were no different from the daily challenges of living in a wheelchair. The skills were totally transferable. Like basketball, life is full of challenges, flagrant fouls and Harrington rods, where the momentum changes all the time.

But the principles of success one can learn—what I learned—on the basketball court translate to life and transcend time and circumstances: Live in each play. Win each play. When the day was over, if I could say I left it all on the court—whatever the outcome—I'd be satisfied.

I couldn't turn my gifts off and on, because it was who I was. God-given gifts and talents will surface in whatever arena you are operating in. It's who you really are, and it was who I really was. So whether I was cross-selling products to an existing customer or coaching with the Vic Tanny Warriors, I was the same person with the same gifts. I felt proud of my contributions in both areas.

My ability to build relationships and make connections quickly with people was also instrumental in my banking career. My responsibilities increased at work as accounts were transferred to me and as I was being added to other accounts as a secondary contact. I had also brought in some new business. I was contributing to the bank's bottom line, and that felt good.

In the spring of 1991, as I approached the completion of my fifth year at the bank, I was rewarded for my work and achieved my goal of becoming a commercial loan officer.

It was with mixed emotions that I resigned from M&I Bank in June of that year. It was time for me to move on. I would be trading in my three-button suits for blue jeans and polo shirts as I pursued my next professional goal: earning an MBA at a top-tier business university.

MY PHOTO ALBUM

Fifth-grade art project, and my parents, Cremella and Jesse Cooks

Freshman year track team photo, the author front and center (April 1979)

David Cooks: courage and attitude exemplory

By Gary Mueller

"Toss it here," shouted a teammate of sophomore David Cooks. "No way, I'll take this one," retorted David.

David took two quick dribbles, faked to the baseline, and fired a twenty foot jumper at the basketball hoop. Swooosh.

"Nice shot, Cookie," a friend yelled.

Sophomore basketball tryouts were only two days away for young David Cooks and the pressure was evident. He could feel it. His legs felt as if they had been asleep for weeks and his back hurt considerably. But was it only pressure?

Sure, he thought to himself Saturday night, as he went to bed. It's probably just something that I ate. At least it's nothing that a good night's sleep won't cure. But was it?

Sunday the legs grew worse. They were wobbly and unsure. The pain intensified, but again he shrugged it off and went to sleep. But as his head hit the pillow, little did he know that when he would awake his life would change dramatically.

Around midnight he awoke, forcing his legs over the side of the bed. He stood up. Crash. Suddenly his legs could not support him. His mind raced as he lay helplessly on the floor. The thought of paralysis rushed through his head first, but he expelled such notions as quickly as they had entered. Afterall, tryouts were the next day.

Immediately, David was rushed to a doctor for examination. By this time, a wheelchair was necessary, and time was running out.

Five hours later, at 5:30 on Monday morning, Dave was admitted at St. Michaels Hospital in Milwaukee. At this point he could no longer feel the pins that the doctors continued to probe his legs with. Specialists were also called in to help try diagnose the problem that seemed to leave everyone baffled. Tests were administered and finally a Milogram was given to determine if there was any blockage around the spine.

There was. A tiny blood vessel that did not have room enough to expand was pressed up against the spinal cord and denying David the use of his legs. It was the first such case any of the doctors had seen. Emergency exploratory surgery was immediately ordered.

Five more long hours passed for David during surgery, until finally, the blood vessel popped out from the spine. It was all over. Surgery was halted. Nothing more could be done. At age 16, young David Cooks was paralyzed from the waist down. There would be no recovery.

Paralysis . . . Crippled . . . Handicapped . . . Such terms would cause most people to shudder. For 17 year old senior David Cooks however, these words mean a way of life. They mean never being able to run across a basketball court. They mean never dancing at the school dance. At times they mean frustration and always they mean dependence. Most of all it means never taking for granted the simple things in life, such as walking and exercising our limbs.

You see, David is paralyzed from the waist down.

And it's because of one simple little blood vessel that didn't have room enough to grow and was pushing up against the spinal cord. There is no medical name for such a problem, since David seems to hold the patent on it and there is no cure. The result? Life in a wheelchair.

Such an existence could quite easily prove devastating, but, fortunately for David, it has not. Young David has certainly not given up, partly due to his lengthy hospital stay immediately following his paralysis.

"When I was in the hospital, I looked around at all the other patients, and after I saw all the people that were worse off than me, I figured I was lucky. It gave me an appreciation for what I do have."

Of course, life in a wheelchair is not all peaches and cream, and David, better than anyone else, knows the feelings of frustration. Getting stuck in the school elevator between the second and third floors was certainly no picnic, and throw in three flat tires that his chair has already suffered this year and you have the makings of a big headache. But, of course, these are only the mechanical problems, and these idiosyncrasies mean relatively little compared to the thought of being dependent on other people forever.

Independence is something that people have fought and even died for, and it's importance to a young man growing up is great. But again David has learned to live with it.

"Sure, there are frustrating times At times it's a real pain, because my dependency on another person can be rather bothersome. Those are the times that you wish you could walk. But it's not the worst."

David's bright outlook on life can best be attested to the support that he received from students, faculty and family. But the biggest source of strength and hope for David is his renewed interest in God. As a born again Christian, he believes that it all comes down to faith in Christ's ability and willingness to help.

"That's what keeps me going from day to day. I figure if He can get the world to rotate 365 days a year then this should be a pushover. Christ has kept me from being depressed."

Those who know David, know that he is one of a kind. His courage is exemplory, and if his future is anything like his positive attitude dictates that it will be, then it should be a happy one. David Cooks is a modern day hero, in his own right.

"It hasn't hit me yet that I'm paralyzed, and it probably never will."

David Cooks lends a smile.

High school newspaper article (Spring 1980)

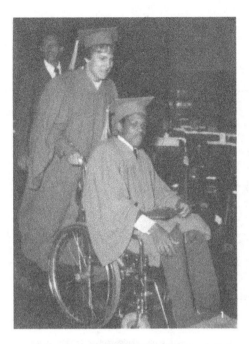

High school graduation with
Jim Van Eerden (May 1982)

Wheelchair basketball (1985)

UW-Whitewater Rolling Warhawks team picture (1984-85 season)

"Morning Inspiration" radio studio at UW-Whitewater

"Morning Inspiration" award

College graduation, May 10, 1986

Charity game photo with Terry Cummings and Michael Jordan (1989)

Vic Tanny Warriors Team in Las Vegas (July 1991)

Vic Tanny Warrior players off the court

Banking mentor Harry Metrusias, his son Chris, and the author (1991)

Frailty of life influences Cooks' positive difference

BOB CHICK

ST. PETERSBURG — Only a minute or so remained in the game when a voice along the sideline called out, "I'm ready, coach," he said as he cupped his hands to his mouth.

The time had come for such requests. Milwaukee owned a 15-point lead against Virginia in this medal round basketball game of the AAU Junior Olympic Games, and David Cooks wanted in.

For one thing Cooks was out of uniform. He wore maroon. Milwaukee was dressed in blue and white. For another, he is a college graduate, commercial banker and at age 25 ineligible for a 19-under tournament.

More important, Cooks, a rugged 6-footer with well defined upper arms, brought his own chair.

In Games that celebrated the joy of athletics, and the bountiful energies of those ages 8-to-18, Cooks was a reminder to the frailty of the human body and why each sunrise should be special.

Talented youth

As a young Milwaukee high school student with enormous athletic talent, he had been tagged by his friends "Gus Williams" after the NBA star. Kids do that, of course. It is an official recognition talent.

Two days before basketball tryouts his sophomore year, Oct. 22, 1979, Cooks had trouble getting out of bed. His legs felt strange, as if they were asleep. By nightfall he was in a wheelchair.

Tests followed, but the decision was final. He'd remain in the chair. The cause: a spinal aneurysm. Damage was irreversible. There had been no virus, no outward signs.

A medical sentence had taken away the use of his legs, even though he fully believes he'll walk again. No one has taken away his heart or spirit.

Maybe in the scheme of things, the David Cooks are a reminder to the rest of us as to how fortunate we are. Cooks never said what happened to him was fair, but he is deeper than that, deeper than the surface of a man in a wheelchair.

He arrived with the Milwaukee basketball team because the coaches and the players wanted him around. His personality is wrapped in so much hope and cheer its upbeat blanket covers those around him.

"I try to feed them (the players) positive things," he said. "Something like a pat on the back, something that will give them purpose. I plant the seeds. I want them to get a grip on education and moral standards and living above the crowd."

Milwaukee coach Tim Larkin calls him one of the most positive individuals he has ever met. Some might see it a bit more. Yet Cooks won't take it the next step, the obvious step.

"I don't like to be considered a role model," he said. "That idea makes me uncomfortable. A role model is not something you touch and feel. A role model is put up on a pedestal all alone, not down with the people. I want to be where they are. I was these players and everyone else to know I support them as a person."

No easy out

No one becomes part of a group without effort. A wheelchair isn't a ticket; respect isn't a given. He has earned his way on to this team, simply because he comes across as a real person who cares and carries himself the way others wished they carried themselves.

"The business of living is a people business. All I can do is offer them the best I can. I try to motivate them, I don't try to inspire them. Inspiration is a big responsibility."

Cooks reaches these heights by being himself. His faith has carried him, a faith that is the resource for all the courage and all the fight he shines everywhere. That plus a strong family and a network of friends.

This is the same light he carries with him in Milwaukee and the surrounding communities. He is on the board of directors of the Fellowship of Christian Athletes. He's a camp director for BAWL - Basketball and a Winning Life, works with Artreach, a program that brings the art, theater and symphony to the disabled and elderly. He has preached at an Assembly of God church. He has also been a peer counselor for those with spinal cord injuries.

"I want my life to be substantial," he said. "I want people to say when I am gone he always gave his 110 percent and did something worthwhile. I feel I have something to offer. Everyone has something, even if it a handshake, hello or a smile."

David Cooks is all of that, too.

Newspaper article given to Coach K by Tommy Amaker

DUKE BASKETBALL

Date __1 Nov '92__   Practice No. _1_

Daily Practice Schedule

TIME: ACTIVITY:

8:45 - 9:15   Pre-Practice __Locker Room - Bring__
                    __Breakfast Food__
              __- Shooting Available__
              __(T.V. on the Court)__ Portable TV on
9:15 - 9:30   STRETCH - Warm!   Players Side
                                  Video on Players Side
9:30 - 9:35   Mike Brey - Talk - conditioning drills + Full-court drill
9:35 - 9:45   Cond. Drills - suicides, jump ropes, def. slides,
                    "14 across", sprint-jog, zig-zag run
9:45 - 10:00   Full Court Drills - 2 Man Drills, 4 Coach Passing,
                    3 Man Passing to F.B., 3 Man Weave to F.B., 3 on 2 to 2 on 1 Rush
10:00 - 10:05 Coach K - Talk - 1st Day Practice - things to look for   Drill
10:05 - 10:15 3 Baskets - Catch + Face (Tony M., Cherokee + Erik Flash w/p
                    - 2 on 0 Screening (Returns - 2 Screeners) (backpicks) 1 Basket)
10:15 - 10:25 2 Baskets - 2 on 2 Screening (Explain Rules)
(Video) 10:25 - 10:30   4 on 4 -
10:30 - 10:35 Talk - T.V. on Ct. - Show Players (bring tape down)
10:35 - 10:40 Zig-Zag   "   Reg -
10:40 - 10:45 3 Baskets - Driving Line - (3 Dribbles) Rt. Side of Basket
10:45 - 10:50 3 Baskets - Contest - Driving Line
10:50 - 11:00 2 Baskets - 2 Man Contesting
(Video) 11:00 - 11:05   4 on 4 -
11:05 - 11:10 Watch Tape
11:10 - 11:15 4 on 4
11:15 - 11:20 Talk - Drills for Per. Players - (Timmy)
Notes: 11:20 - 11:35   Offense
11:35 - 11:45   ← 4 Spot Shooting
11:45 - 12:00   6 Pt. Contesting - 3 on 3 Full Court on Def. Reb.
12:00 - 12:30   (Pete) Keep your best scorer involved in
                    the Offense -

The practice plan from the first Duke practice I attended

Manager teaches players about life, basketball

Cooks' daily challenge of life similar to days on court

1993 ACC Tournament article

Talking with Coach
Dean Smith and
Phil Ford
before the Duke vs
UNC game
(Feb. 3, 1993)

Fuqua School of
Business graduation
(May 15, 1993

Fuqua School
Commencement Address

My Photo Album

My family at Business
School graduation

Picture with Duke Basketball
players after final dinner in
Durham, NC

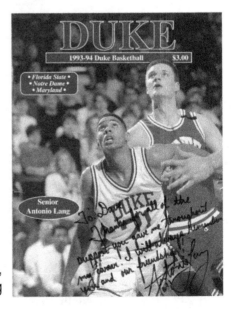

Duke Basketball game program,
autographed by Tony Lang

Article from Darien newspaper on hiring me (1994)

Action coaching picture from
Darien newspaper

DUKE UNIVERSITY BASKETBALL
CAMERON INDOOR STADIUM · BOX 10556 · DURHAM, NORTH CAROLINA 27708-0556

June 6, 1994

Coach Dave Cooks
c/o Darien High School
80 High School Lane
Darien, Ct. 06820

Dear Dave:

Congratulations on being named the new head basketball coach at Darien High School. We are very excited and thrilled to know that you are back in coaching and doing something that you really enjoy and that you are really good at. The whole Duke coaching staff is extremely proud to of played a small part in your being named the new head basketball coach.

We want you to know that at this point whenever you get your first blue chip basketball recruit that we expect him to be signed, sealed, and delivered to Duke University.

Once again, congratulations and take care.

Sincerely,

Congrats!
Tommy

What a Great Choice!
Good Luck, Buddy!!
Coach K.

Way to go —
now you need some
transfers from Nigeria!
Mike B

yes! Pete Gaudet

Congratulatory letter from Duke Coaching Staff

My first varsity team at Darian

Coach K and me at Duke
Coaches Clinic

Stamford Express visits Milwaukee (1995)

Stamford Express Championship Team

Our wedding, August 18, 2007

With MariPat's parents

With my parents

Our combined families

Marquette University High School alumni

Plaid Shirt Monday at Marquette University High School

WIAA 2010 Sectional Champs

2010 WIAA state tournament

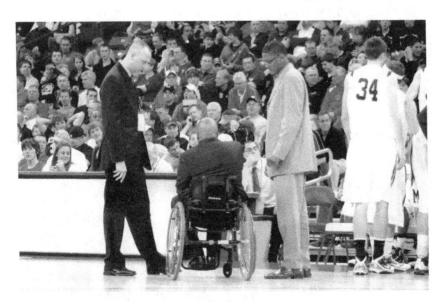

My assistant coaches, Mark Briggs and Neil O'Connell,
at the 2010 WIAA state tournament

My final basketball senior class: Tom Enright, Andy Krueger, AJ Meuller, TJ Novotny, Tom Beres, Alex McBride (Feb. 2013)

An evening of gratitude at MUHS

My Photo Album

USA East Coast Basketball team, Columbia University training camp
(August 2014)

USA East Coast versus Austria rosters

Marquette University High School
commencement address (2014)

Former players John Kopriva and Quinten Calloway from
the 2010 WIAA State Tournament team

Building Bridges student award night (2016)

Building Bridges parents (2016)

MUHS Freshman retreat (2017)

A parting gift from a student

Chapter 9: Persistence

Duke Basketball: Meeting Coach K

When you have a goal, when you have a dream,
when you have a passion for something, don't let it go easily.

STANFORD UNIVERSITY WAS AT THE TOP OF my list for graduate schools to attend. I didn't get accepted as an undergraduate applicant, but that didn't deter me from trying again. Northwestern, North Carolina, Duke, and Texas were also universities on my radar.

I had established the following criteria when identifying potential graduate programs: 1) consistently ranked in the top ten nationally; 2) Division I basketball program, and 3) warm weather (with the exception of Northwestern University).

Once again, I was denied admission to Stanford University; however, I received phone calls from Northwestern and Duke requesting that I schedule campus visits as a final step in their admissions processes. The final decision would come down to what best suited me.

My first stop was Northwestern University. The visit was on a beautiful June summer day in Chicago along the lakefront, but thoughts of making my way to class through the snow, ice, wind, and sleet of Chicago winters made me pause.

The longer I was in a wheelchair, the more important convenience and ease became. If I didn't have to struggle through something, why should I? From an academic perspective, there was no additional benefit for me to suffer through Chicago winters. It wasn't that I couldn't handle it—I had done it for four years at Whitewater—but if I had other options that would make my experience outside the classroom more palatable, I would be foolish not to consider it. Before accepting Northwestern's offer, I needed to visit Duke University.

A week later, I flew to the Fuqua School of Business at Duke University in Durham, North Carolina. Shortly into my interview, I learned what drew their attention to my application. It was my response to the following question: Describe your ideal job. It was a pretty general question, but it didn't take me long to write "coaching basketball in a town of lakes."

You see, I didn't know any better than to tell the truth. They said they found my response refreshing, out-of-the-box and honest. They appreciated how my response reflected what I was really thinking and not what I thought they wanted me to say. I could have lied and said that, too, but if I could coach, fish and make a good living, why wouldn't I?

The second thing that stood out to me—other than the beauty of the campus—was how nice the people were; it must have been their southern hospitality. If accepted, I would be the first full-time student in a wheelchair to attend the Fuqua School of Business.

Being the first at things was something I had grown accustomed to. The further I advanced in my education and professional career, the more I observed that I was often the first and the only person in a wheelchair and of African American descent in the room. Being the only one wasn't a negative; it was something I leveraged to break down myths, stereotypes and misperceptions—both racially and physically.

Being the first through the door—so to speak—allowed me to keep the door open for those coming behind me who were like me.

The interview ended, and I was offered admission into the Fuqua School of Business Class of 1993. I was also awarded a fellowship grant as part of the admissions package. I thanked them and told them I needed a few days to weigh my options.

It didn't take long. I decided to go to Duke.

Durham, North Carolina would be my new home away from home for the next two years. Now that my professional goal of earning my MBA was in order, for the rest of that summer, my love for basketball had me asking myself a question: Could I do something with it at Duke?

Coaching with the Vic Tanny Warriors had stirred my interest in staying connected with the game I loved. The years I spent with that team made me comfortable interacting with college coaches at every level. The fact that players in the program went on to play at the likes of Kansas, Northwestern, Vanderbilt, Utah and Wisconsin made the prospect of being part of Duke basketball a little less daunting. I'd need to rely on all those experiences if I was to accomplish step one toward my goal: winning a meeting with Duke men's basketball coach Mike Krzyzewski.

I arrived on campus in August of 1991—a couple of weeks prior to classes beginning. Once I got settled in my apartment on University Avenue, I headed over to Cameron Indoor Stadium in hopes of introducing myself to "Coach K."

Admittedly, trying to meet Coach K was on a different level than my past experiences. But then again, what did I have to lose? I was going to be there for two years anyway—and if I was turned away, I'd still enjoy being a fan at sporting events while I received a world-class education.

When I rolled into Cameron Indoor Stadium for the first time, there in the ticket lobby was the 1991 National Championship trophy and net from the title game. DUKE 77, KANSAS 65. Behind it were images from their magical run, including the alley-oop pass Grant Hill threw down in the first half of the championship. What would I have given to have been at that game?

I left the lobby and headed into the gym. It wasn't as large as I expected, but it was Duke. I was at Duke. In Cameron Indoor Stadium. Where it all happens—where Hurley, Laettner, Davis, Clark, Lang, Thomas Hill, Grant Hill and the rest of the team put their work in. There, up in the rafters behind the basket on the east end of court was the 1991 NCAA National Championship banner. It had a magical presence even without the undergraduate student fans (the "Cameron Crazies") and thousands of other fans screaming at the top of their lungs.

But where was Coach K's office?

I left the court and headed back toward the lobby, looking for signage that would direct me to the men's basketball office. Just before I re-entered the lobby, I saw a door to my right. I went through that door and took a right. There was a long hallway with pictures of Duke men's basketball teams framed on the walls in black and white and in color. I rolled down that hallway peeping into offices as I passed by; none were for men's basketball. I figured it must be somewhere else. I found an exit sign at the end of the hall and headed toward that. As I approached, there was one more office up on the left that I could check. And someone was at the front desk.

"Can you tell me where the men's basketball offices are?" I asked.

"This is the men's basketball office," the woman behind the counter said. "How can I help you?"

My pulse raced, and my hands started to sweat. "My name is David Cooks. I'm a grad student at the Fuqua School of Business. I'm from Wisconsin. I love basketball, and I wanted to see if I could meet with Coach K?"

I stammered my way through that and wished I could have made a slightly more positive first impression.

"Coach K is on vacation," she replied. "He's not here, but I can leave a message for him if you'd like."

She jotted my name down on a pink standard message form— the same ones I used at the bank—and she put it on a mailbox shelf.

"My name's Donna. It was nice to meet you, David."

"Nice meeting you, too."

I turned to leave, but something was gnawing at the back of my mind: Was Coach K really on vacation? Or was this what she told everyone who inquired about him? If I did get blown off, at least she did it in the nicest way possible. And she never said I couldn't meet him, so I still had a chance. I decided to return in a few days.

When I did, I was told the same thing and left the same message as before. Classes were quickly approaching. I wanted to see this through before my coursework received my undivided attention. I decided I'd give it one more shot. And if it proved fruitless a third time, I could move on knowing it wasn't from a lack of trying.

Less than a week before school, I returned to the men's basketball offices—but this time, Donna told me something different: He wasn't in his office at the moment.

"Does that mean he's back from vacation?" I asked excitedly.

"Yes, he is."

"Okay, I'll come back."

I opened the office door to leave and—

"Hey! Aren't you that guy from Wisconsin?"

I was from Wisconsin, but was I that guy from Wisconsin? I stopped in my tracks and spun around to see who had said it. It looked like someone who played for Duke.

"Yes, I'm from Wisconsin. Who are you?"

"Tony Lang. I remember seeing you down in St. Petersburg, Florida with your AAU team from Wisconsin. You guys had Damon Key on your team, right?"

"Yeah," I said, trying to jog my memory back to that tournament. We played so many games in so many cities. I remembered we opened against Chris Webber's AAU team, but that was about it.

"I loved the way you worked with your guys. You gonna help us out this year?"

I nearly jumped out of my seat. "I sure hope so."

Here's Tony Lang saying this outside of Coach K's office in front of people who could help me meet him. I had never received a timelier and more satisfying recommendation in my life. It came from a total stranger who simply noticed me going about my business. It was a foot in the door, but that didn't mean I was in.

Later that afternoon, I stopped by the Fuqua School of Business to set up my email account and get better acquainted with WordPerfect and Microsoft Excel. As I made my way to the elevator, I spotted none other than Coach Tommy Amaker, the Duke point guard from 1983 to 1987, leaving the building.

I met him at the bottom of the stairs and introduced myself, explained my failed attempts at meeting Coach K, and offered my help in whatever capacity the team needed. Tommy asked if I had a resume or anything he could give Coach K on my behalf. I rifled through my briefcase and found at the bottom of it a newspaper article from The Tampa Tribune written by Bob Chick: "Frailty of Life Influences Cooks' Positive Difference." Ironically enough, Chick published it when the AAU tournament in St. Petersburg was going on; yes, the very same tournament Tony had referenced earlier that day in the men's basketball offices.

Destiny was on my side once again. It wasn't like I walked around town with articles about me in my briefcase. It was the only copy of the article I owned. I didn't hesitate to give it to Coach Amaker, but thankfully, he was the voice of reason in my haste and suggested we go inside to make a copy for him. It wasn't a resume, but it would have to do. Most importantly, he promised to get it into Coach K's hands.

A few moments after he left and I regained my wits, I realized I had committed a cardinal sin when interviewing for a job: I left without establishing a follow-up action step. I never gave him a way to get in contact with me again, nor did I ask what would be the best way to get a hold of him. I guessed it would be up to me to make another trip back to Cameron, but I decided I'd wait a few days.

The semester was scheduled to begin after Labor Day, so I figured I'd pay what I hoped to be my final visit to the men's basketball offices the Friday before school started. I parked near the outdoor basketball courts, across from the baseball field, and started to make my way toward Cameron.

As I headed down the hill toward the stadium, I spotted him: Coach K. It was unmistakable. I cranked my wheels harder than I've ever done before, flying down the hill at a dangerous pace. I've gotta meet him. I've gotta meet him.

We met at the entrance. Despite being winded, I managed not to stumble over my words.

"Hi, Coach K. I'm David Cooks and—"

"I know who you are," he interrupted. "I read the article Coach Amaker gave me, and I've been wanting to meet with you. Did you have time to meet right now?"

Did I have time?! I couldn't get the "yes" out fast enough.

We went into his office, and he laid out his dilemma. He was interested in me joining the program, but he was fully staffed. Jay Bilas, author and ESPN analyst, was their graduate assistant completing his law degree. Tommy Amaker, current Harvard University head coach, and Mike Brey, Notre Dame head coach, were assistant coaches alongside top assistant Pete Gaudet. Even the manager positions were filled for the upcoming year. Simply put, there weren't any openings.

Yet I still wanted to be part of the program. I said I'd do anything. Coach K wasn't sure what I could do or what there was for me to do, but he graciously offered me access to their practices to observe.

I accepted his invitation.

Chapter 10: Pride

Duke Basketball: Filling Water Bottles

Take advantage of whatever opportunity you're given.
How you handle success will determine
how much success you can handle.

WHEN I INFORMED THE ADMINISTRATION at the business school that I was going to be working with the Duke basketball program while taking classes toward my degree, their response was lukewarm. It hadn't been done before...and with the wheelchair...they were concerned.

But I wasn't. It was a choice of mine. A tradeoff. Instead of wasting three or four hours per day on other, non-academic things—which I knew I'd do—I wanted to spend that time on basketball. Did it mean my weekends were going to be filled with more coursework? Of course it did. It didn't mean it couldn't be done, though. Being the first to do something wasn't intimidating to me.

I took advantage of the first month and a half of classes to get off to a solid academic start and to establish a routine. If I was going to be successful academically, I was going to have to learn from my classmates. I was no longer always the smartest person in the room. I couldn't run away from that fact. I had to step up my game.

Getting Undressed

On October 15, 1991, I attended the first Duke practice. I arrived at Cameron Indoor Stadium about 45 minutes early. I'm still not quite sure why I was so nervous, considering I was merely spectating, but I was. One of the managers handed me a practice plan, which had every minute accounted for in their two-hour workout.

I didn't want to distract or get in the way, so I sat on the baseline near the locker rooms by the Gatorade jugs and ball racks. One by one, the athletes stopped and introduced themselves to me during pre-practice stretching. I didn't expect that, but I came to learn that was part of the Blue Devil culture Coach K taught his players.

Practice was intense—a reflection of Coach K. Lots of talking. Lots of teaching. Lots of competing. I paid special attention to how the players interacted with each other and the coaches. There were three things that stood out about Coach K that went beyond his mastery of the X's and O's of the game: his standards, his preparation and his communication. Each reflected his unwavering commitment to excellence.

I later learned that on day one of practice, Coach K reiterated clear standards for the program—both on and off the court, and in and out of season. With these expectations came accountability on a personal and team level. Coach K wouldn't settle for anything less than the team's individual and collective best. Everyone—including the coaches—was expected to look in the mirror and assess his effort and contribution to the greater goal. Finger pointing wasn't tolerated within that culture.

As I continued to attend practices, I continued to be amazed by Coach K's preparation. It was like nothing I'd ever seen before.

His attention to detail was borderline compulsive for me, but I saw the benefits of putting the team in a position to handle whatever obstacles came their way. Playing at Duke put a target on a lot of those players' backs. Every team was gunning for them. Coach K understood the value of being able to rely on fundamentals, established through preparation, in order to get through the adverse moments of a game or season.

Coach K's communication (and not just his talking) is what separated him from his peers. Coach K had a keen sense of which buttons to push for each player and when to push them. It was like he knew how his players would respond before he spoke. It was never a cookie-cutter approach. He genuinely cared about the well-being of every player on the roster, and when a player at any level can sense that, they'll give their maximum effort and commitment. It's how you build lasting relationships.

The coaching staff reinforced the constant need for effective communication on and off the court. It sometimes required a few corrective measures in the heat of competition, but it always remained honest and respectful—whether you were a player or coach. What one said verbally and nonverbally mattered. Coach K's culture made it possible to be demanding without being demeaning. Everybody in the program wanted to win, but never at the cost of personal or collective integrity.

It was a busy fall for me, as I made every practice and continued the MBA grind. It was books and Duke basketball exclusively—except for November 7, 1991, when Magic Johnson announced he had contracted HIV. For a moment, Duke basketball was not the topic of conversation in our study group.

Getting Undressed

As much as I enjoyed the daily practices, there was nothing like game day in Cameron Indoor Stadium. The lines and tents outside. The Cameron Crazies. The Blue Devil Mascot. The creative cheers from the student section. The overall energy inside the building made each and every game its own great experience.

I attended every home game and as many road games as I could. My only regret was not attending the Duke-Kentucky Regional Final game at the Spectrum in Philadelphia—I had an early flight the next morning to head back to Wisconsin for an internship interview with Midwest Express Airlines. Like millions of others, I watched on TV as Christian Laettner make "the shot" at the buzzer, putting the Blue Devils into the Final Four—and putting that game in NCAA infamy forever. To add insult to injury, I didn't get the summer internship with Midwest Express Airlines; I did, however, enjoy the wide leather seats and homemade chocolate chip cookies on the flights to and from Wisconsin.

As soon as I returned to Durham, I didn't hesitate to let Coach K know that I'd be on the flight to Minneapolis for the Final Four. I had grown accustomed to the rock band-like following the team had wherever we went, but the attention at the Final Four was in another stratosphere. I was even asked for autographs and photo ops. The environment was electrifying.

The ability for the team to stay focused and on task in a distraction-filled environment was impressive. Coach K did not change anything in terms of how the team practiced and prepared for the semifinal game against Indiana University and legendary coach Bob Knight, nor the final game against the University of Michigan. It was Duke's 3rd consecutive Final Four, and they treated it like a business trip until the work was completed. Duke beat Michigan's "Fab 5" team 71-51 in the National Championship game to become back-to-back champs.

The season had come to an end, and for the next month and a half, I had to refocus solely on my academics. I needed to finish strong and prepare for the summer internship I was offered with GE Capital in Stamford, Connecticut—an hour north of New York City.

New York City was a 45-minute train ride from Stamford, which allowed me to experience a lot of what New York City had to offer: Times Square, Wall Street, the Statue of Liberty, the Metropolitan Museum of Art, Sparks Steakhouse and Sylvia's in Harlem. While most people would see these on foot, I did so on wheels. I didn't take a cab. I rolled from Grand Central Station to South Street Seaport, making stops everywhere in between, there and back.

My summer with GE Capital was fabulous. I wanted to use my internship as an opportunity to interview them as much as they were interviewing me. I wanted to see if the culture, the people and the work were consistent with what I wanted to do. I wasn't sure where I wanted to go with my MBA, other than to consider a position in management within a professional sports organization.

GE passed the test. I liked the work, the people and my overall experience that summer. I returned to Durham ready to complete my MBA and to rejoin the Duke basketball program after a great summer gaining professional experience.

Shortly after school began that fall, I met with Coach K, and he offered me a manager's position with the program. There I was, a 28-year-old graduate student working towards my MBA, being offered a job reserved for undergraduates. That wasn't what I was expecting. I had hoped to replace Jay Bilas as the Graduate Assistant, but that position wasn't available.

In that moment, I had to decide whether or not I would accept the role offered to me. If what Coach K offered me offended me and I didn't accept the offer, the opportunity to be in the program would be eliminated. I could either be part of the program or be excluded from it.

Pride can close the door on opportunities, whereas humility can keep them open. I could remain humble and get involved, or I could let my ego get the better of me and not get involved. At what cost was I willing to be part of this program? How much was I willing to pay to do this?

The reason I said yes to Coach K was because I had the endgame in mind. This was a once-in-a-lifetime opportunity to learn the game and learn my passion from inside one of the best college basketball programs in America—and from one of the greatest coaches of all time. How could I refuse?

I accepted his offer to be a manager in the Duke basketball program.

I didn't have to wait for the players to arrive at practice to officially begin. There were many preseason meetings, where veteran managers showed neophytes like me the ropes. By the time the season began on November 1, I was ready to go.

I found myself filling water bottles, chasing down loose balls, doing the players' laundry, barking out encouragements, and doing anything the coaches asked of me. As I did this, I pushed myself to be the best ball-shagger and Gatorade brewer on the team. It must have been my Wisconsin roots kicking in. I wasn't just a manager. I was a manager helping the team win. That was my perspective.

Everything was important, whether it was filling water bottles or executing the full court trap. Cutting corners wasn't an option—especially within Coach K's culture. There was purpose in the process, and the attitude I took going into each task mattered as much as the outcome. I learned to do one thing at a time, the right way, and give each experience my full attention. I was committed to doing everything with excellence—yes, even if my task was filling water bottles.

Coach K took notice.

In addition to my duties as a manager, I had also been able to talk game strategy with the coaching staff. In Coach K's words, which I heard later on, "eventually they realized I knew a little something about the game." He began including me on film sessions, coach meetings and player workouts, and I was given an increased role in helping to coach in practices. I even had the pleasure of periodically addressing the team. I was still a manager, but I had been given a promotion of sorts. Just like Tony Lang in St. Petersburg, Coach K observed my persistence, my dedication, my punctuality and my attention to detail—completely unbeknownst to me.

The players took notice, too.

Thanks to Bobby Hurley and Chris Collins, I became known amongst the team as "Scooks." It was a term of endearment. To them, I had become a part-time coach, part-time psychiatrist and part-time teacher, because I mentored players in everything basketball, breakups and business. I got to know these players—this family—on an intimate level.

My persistence made me part of the program, and Coach K and the players made me part of the Duke family.

My final game as a Duke manager happened when I was out of town, watching Duke on TV in the Sweet 16 game against California. Quite frankly, I thought they'd win—but Jason Kidd and company had other plans. The season, for both the team and for me, came to an abrupt end. I was going to miss my pregame ritual of getting a hug from Coach K's 12-year-old daughter Jamie, meals at Bullock's, and interacting with the players and staff. The games, the practices and the travel were all great, but as it is with anything, it's the people who made the difference.

At the end-of-year banquet, Coach K publicly thanked me for my contributions to the program. Grant Hill, Erik Meek, Marty Clark, Tony Lang, Stanley Brunson and Kenny Blakeney expressed their gratitude in the form of a going-away party at Kyoto's Japanese Steakhouse.

I considered myself one of the most fortunate people on the planet. It made me realize that you never know who's watching and where your next connection may come from. I learned to not despise small beginnings; they can lead to really big endings—like going from the playgrounds of Milwaukee to Cameron Indoor Stadium.

There wasn't an opportunity for me to coach on Duke's staff the next year, and since I completed my MBA and would no longer be a student there, it was time to move on.

But not before addressing our class, faculty, family, and friends at the graduation ceremony in Cameron Indoor Stadium—and receiving a standing ovation—in May of 1993.

Upon graduating, I accepted a full-time position with GE Capital in Stamford, Connecticut. It was time to get undressed once more. I needed to purchase some new suits.

Chapter 11: Patience

Building a Winning Culture

A winning culture has little to do with wins or losses and everything to do with preparation, attitude and effort.

MY FIRST ASSIGNMENT AS AN ASSOCIATE at GE Capital was underwriting loans in their commercial aviation division. It involved a lot of financial modeling for companies looking to lease and acquire aircraft. Deals varied in size and complexity, with the largest deal I helped underwrite going for one billion dollars.

The job required a lot of traveling. I always looked forward to my time in Cincinnati and Houston—especially for the cuisine. I wasn't a fan of Skyline Chili in Cincinnati, but the Waterfront Seafood Restaurant (Chart House) on the Ohio-Kentucky border was always satisfying. And in Houston, it was all about the barbeque.

As much as I loved the work and its perks, it didn't take long for me to realize I'd need to be intentional about developing a work-life balance. During the interviewing process with GE Capital, I made it perfectly clear that I was planning on getting involved with basketball in the area. Basketball would serve as my community service. Still, if I wasn't careful, GE Capital could totally consume my life. I had to protect my life outside of work.

A few months into the job, I called several high school basketball coaches and athletic directors in the area to volunteer my help in whatever capacity they needed. I didn't mention my two years of Duke experience, nor did I mention my AAU experience in Wisconsin. All I told them was that I was new to the area, worked for GE Capital, and looked to get involved in basketball.

One by one, my enthusiastic phone calls were met with definitive "no's," until Coach Jim Moriarty, the boys' head basketball coach at Stamford High School, accepted my offer. For the 1993-1994 season, I volunteered with the Stamford High School program.

Stamford High School is an urban high school located in the heart of Stamford, Connecticut. Coach Moriarty used his engaging smile, laugh and personality to help his players navigate through difficult life situations. He was an excellent coach, and one who inspired me to think larger than volunteering with basketball programs—specifically, that maybe I could be a head coach and lead a program of my own.

There was one glaring problem, though: I had a well-paying, full-time job that often required me to leave the area for days or weeks on end. The business world wouldn't stop if I had basketball games or practices. As a volunteer, I could attend practices and games on an "as available" basis. As a high school head coach, I would need to be there every day with the players. How feasible would it be to underwrite multi-million dollar loans by day and lead a basketball program by night?

Partway through the 1993-1994 season, I talked with Coach Moriarty about starting an AAU team in Fairfield County, Connecticut. There were a couple of established and nationally recognized AAU programs already in Southeastern Connecticut—including the Connecticut Select, led by Wayne Simone, and the Cardinal Shehan Center, led by Brad Shapiro—but they traditionally only worked with the best players in the area, mainly the Division I scholarship-level players.

So what about the other players—the non-scholarship-level players—wanting to continue playing at least another four years? Where could they play during the summers? Who was helping them?

Why not me?

It would be a perfect opportunity for me to get my feet wet with head coaching while still preserving my professional career at GE Capital. Coach Moriarty thought it was a good idea, too, and he was willing to help find gym time and spread the word to other coaches in the Fairfield County Interscholastic Athletic Conference (FCIAC).

The Stamford Express AAU basketball program was born, with its official launch set for the spring of 1994. The team's mission was to develop young men as people and as basketball players through instruction, competition and mentoring. Next, I needed to find other coaches who shared my love for the game and for making a positive impact on young people.

Warren Spann, a Wharton MBA and fellow associate at GE Capital within the commercial aviation division, grew close with me during my first year at the company. Warren was a huge basketball fan—and a good player in his own right. He came from Mount Vernon, New York, a city that's produced its fair share of NBA players—including my namesake, Gus Williams. An outstanding evaluator of talent, Warren embraced the Stamford Express mission and accepted my invitation to be an assistant coach for the Express.

Tryouts for this grass-roots team were held up the road from Stamford at Fairfield University. Players throughout the FCIAC and neighboring conferences showed up in droves, but Coach Spann and I were particular about the makeup of our teams. We were looking for players with good character and good ability. From there, we'd look at the position(s) they played.

Given that we'd be spending every weekend of our summer traveling with these players, character was our first priority. We wanted players in the program that we would enjoy being around. We were willing to sacrifice ability for attitude, if it came to that. We were also committed to our teams being diverse—economically and ethnically, urban and suburban, white and black, poor and wealthy. Of course, we needed a good mix of guards, forwards and centers to compete, too—but we were intentional about identifying and selecting off-the-court characteristics as much as we were looking for on-the-court talent.

Tryouts were two hours long, with detailed practice plans accounting for every minute—a trait I learned from Coach K at Duke. The majority of the drills were full court and allowed for us to evaluate the fundamentals of passing, dribbling and shooting. We used scrimmaging to evaluate a player's ability and desire to defend.

After a few weeks, Warren and I made our final cuts and formed our first teams. We guaranteed that every player would participate in at least three local or regional tournaments. At that time, we had no jerseys, no shoes, and no sponsorships. Soon after its inception, I helped establish the Stamford Express Foundation, a 5013c corporation, so fundraisers could donate to the program with a tax write-off. Each player was responsible for paying a $500 fee for the summer, so Coach Warren and I needed to deliver on our promises to the players.

Because of the diversity of our program, this was a first experience away from home for many players. Traveling—which included many hours of listening to audio books in vans and overnight stays in hotels—was an integral part of the Stamford Express experience. Our trips helped bring us together as a team and build relationships. During the winters, they would play on opposing teams. During the summers, they'd be teammates.

Darien High School was one of the other schools in the FCIAC. The Stamford Express had two of its players: Mike Malone and Rob Kennedy. Mike was a point guard who could defend and had great court vision. Rob was a tough, physical, streaky shooting guard who couldn't be stopped when on his game. I remembered competing against them when Stamford High played Darien.

After an AAU practice one day, Mike and Rob approached me because Darien High School was looking for a head coach—a position that had been a revolving door for years. Darien happened to be the first school I randomly contacted about volunteering, and the first to turn me down.

Darien High School had a basketball tradition, but it wasn't a winning one. Darien, a small school with limited basketball talent, was fighting an uphill battle in one of the most competitive conferences in the Northeast. The challenge of turning it around appealed to me. After all, I couldn't do much worse, could I?

I interviewed with Jim Girard, the school's athletic director, for the vacant boys' head coaching position. He was frank about the program's struggles and was looking for someone willing to make a minimum of a three- to five-year commitment in order to bring it to a place of respectability in the FCIAC.

I was willing to do that, but I knew I would need some accommodations. Most importantly, practices would have to be held from 6 p.m. to 8 p.m. That would be the only way I could imagine myself managing work and basketball. I also asked for access to the gym in the summers to run basketball camps and to have practices for the Stamford Express.

Jim smirked at my request.

"Is that all you want?" he said incredulously. "Of course, we can do that."

"You do know that I haven't been a head coach before and that I have a full-time job, right? I'll be an out-of-the-building coach."

"Yes, I'm aware of that," he said. "I've done my homework on you. I've watched some of your AAU practices and games. Mike Malone and Rob Kennedy speak very highly of their overall experience with you. I'd like to offer you the job."

Without asking about the salary, without taking a weekend to think about it, I accepted the offer on the spot. At age 30, I'd be a real head coach for the first time (AAU didn't count in my eyes) in one of the most competitive leagues around.

Almost immediately, I realized I inherited a basketball program that lacked standards, discipline and leadership. Darien basketball was built around one player who was given the green light to basically do whatever he wanted in practices and games.

Sharing the ball and working together as a team was not part of the Darien culture—yet. My job was to turn this culture around before we could address the X's and O's of the game. That had to change first, if we wanted any chance of becoming a respectable program in the FCIAC.

Changing a culture starts with changing the mindset. Each player had to shift how he conducted things, and we needed to feed ourselves the winning habits and skills that we wanted to see come out of us. We couldn't just talk about change; we had to practice it. Change doesn't happen by happenstance. It requires a willingness to confront fear, pain and uncomfortable truths—and the courage, discipline, out-of-the-box thinking and hard work to produce tangible results. Hard work makes people tired, and it can be tedious—but it develops a special kind of work ethic and muscle memory that shows up in critical situations.

A winning culture competes every day, improving individual and collective skill sets. It never marginalizes roles or responsibilities; instead, it stresses the importance of each role in accomplishing universal goals. In a winning culture, each player is expected to work hard, stay prepared, care for one another, make sacrifices and produce when called upon.

Winning and losing have as much to do with talent and the opponent as they do with strategy. To consistently win at any level—in any sport or business—you must have talented players on your roster who embrace the culture of the team or organization. Culture is about the approach; it's about what you do and don't do.

I knew all too well the value of having encouraging influences around me, of finding victories in the midst of what others considered defeat, and of bonding as a team to keep the ship afloat during turbulent times. The players, the parents, the coaches, the administrators—everyone within the program—needed that. Developing trust in each other had to happen first, because without trust, there can be no change.

I was fortunate to have the support of Jim Girard the entire way. In The Darien News Review publication on June 9, 1994 that announced my hiring, he was quoted as saying, "He is very dynamic and has tremendous leadership skills. I went over and observed him coaching in a practice and a game to get a feel for how he handled himself, how he handled kids, and how he handled his disability—which in my opinion is not even a factor. He's a great teacher and earns your respect right away."

Sadly, I didn't always gain the support of everyone at Darien. Darien basketball was nestled between two very successful sports programs: football and lacrosse. To improve the basketball team, I would need those coaches to allow and encourage athletes from their respective sports to join the basketball program. I believed that basketball's success would not take away from the success of other sports teams; rather, it made everyone better athletes overall. I quickly found out I was in the minority on that. Unfortunately, that collaboration never gained sustained traction during my tenure.

My first act as Darien's head coach was to meet with the players who were already a part of the program, as well as any others interested in trying out in the winter. We met in the gym, which appeared to have not been updated for several years. But I framed it as a positive—a home court advantage that might make it a tougher environment for opponents to play in.

Patience

I started by informing the team that we'd be getting new uniforms. We were starting over, and a change of clothes was in order. I shared with them the three things I expected if they were to play: to be hardworking, to be a good teammate, and to be a good citizen. From now on, our motto was going to be "play to win." To do that, it first involved becoming competitive—and that could only happen if we developed the winning habits of discipline, accountability and standards. Then, we'd have to learn how to win and how to handle success. After all, how we handled success would determine how much success we could handle.

It was a positive first step, and the team seemed to take to me and to my message. Now came the tough part: following through with my strategy. At the very least, for the first time in a while, there was a buzz about basketball at Darien. November 28, 1994, the first day of practice, couldn't come fast enough.

Chapter 12: Passion

Taking a Pay Cut

What you are willing to sacrifice today is an indication of its value and where you are trying to go in the future. If it's a priority, sacrifices are made; everything else gets excuses.

BETWEEN GETTING MY NEXT ASSIGNMENT at GE Capital, becoming the boys' head basketball coach at Darien, and launching the Stamford Express, the summer of 1994 had it all for me.

The highlight of our inaugural summer with the Stamford Express was a trip to my hometown of Milwaukee. Many of the guys on the team had no idea where Wisconsin was. We might as well have been going to Spain! But that was part of our process. We sought to provide new experiences for the players, on and off the court, and taking an airplane to Milwaukee would be one of them.

While there, we competed in a tournament at Concordia University in the morning and spent the afternoon and evening at Summerfest, the world's largest music festival, situated on the shores of Lake Michigan. Pearl Jam was the main attraction that day.

The trip ended with a backyard barbeque hosted by my parents at my childhood home. Johnsonville bratwurst filled the grill outside, and Kopp's Frozen Custard was the perfect end to the meal and trip. We gave the kids a taste of what midwest hospitality was all about.

By summer's end, I had completed my rotation in the commercial aviation division at GE Capital. My next assignment was in the power plant workout division, which had a lot more financial modeling and pricing but substantially less customer interaction. The latter didn't appeal to me as much, but I figured I could handle it for the next twelve months. It was only temporary.

One of the most important benefits of my new rotation would be less travel. My supervisors were aware of my Darien head coaching position, and much like at Fuqua, they were lukewarm on the idea—and questioned my commitment to GE Capital.

I reassured them that my first priority would continue to be GE, and what I did after hours would remain after hours. Even if it meant coming in early and returning to the office after practice, I would make this work. Besides, the season wouldn't begin for another three months, which would give me time to adjust to the new responsibilities.

As the season approached, however, I found it harder to keep basketball away from the office. I caught myself mulling over practice schedules, diagramming plays and brainstorming team building exercises when my mind wandered. I wasn't enjoying the new rotation at all. I was all in, but the isolation from customers was taking its toll on me. Internally, I yearned to interact and connect directly with people—the way coaching basketball did. I told myself that it would improve once the season started. Coaching would serve as my respite from the slower winter season and hours of number crunching at the office.

During the fall, I hired my coaching staff. There were four things I looked for in my assistant coaches: character, competence, communication (people skills) and commitment (loyalty). The same standards I had for our players were applicable to the coaches, too. Darien needed coaches who modeled what winning looks like.

Warren Spann, who assisted me with the Stamford Express, was my first hire. I later added Ted Keating, Kyle Rogers and Adam Berkowitz—all from Fairfield County. Each coach brought something different to the table and challenged me to get better every day. I needed that, especially as a first-time head coach. Building a winning culture, and ultimately a championship, starts with sound leadership.

November 28, 1994 had finally arrived. At 6 p.m. that evening, I would be leading my first practice as a high school head coach. I spent most of the day at work watching the clock and looking over the practice plan again and again. I pretty much had it memorized: ball handling, three-man weave, two-man series, 80 layups, partner shooting, two-ball shooting, 11-man fast break, four-man shell, scrimmaging, conditioning, conditioning, conditioning.

I arrived in the gym at 5:30 to meet with my staff. I was hyped and full of energy; they had to be, too. The task before us was daunting, and we needed to approach it enthusiastically and with lots of positive energy. You can only make a first impression once. This was a new beginning for all of us.

This first day of tryouts was our first time to see up close what we inherited. Darien shared the same color scheme as Duke—and we were able to purchase a replica of the Duke jerseys—but the similarities began and ended there. Grant Hill and Marty Clark weren't in the program. Making plays above the rim were few and far between. This wasn't Duke. This wasn't the Stamford Express. This was Darien, home of the Blue Wave, and our job was to work with Darien's players and rebuild the program.

With garbage cans strategically placed throughout the gym and excitement buzzing through the air, we eagerly began tryouts. For three days, players were put through perhaps the most physically and mentally challenging experiences of their young athletic careers. Hard work wasn't rewarded; it was expected. That was the tone we set from day one.

The most difficult part of tryouts was having to make cuts. There's no pleasure in telling young men that they didn't make the team, but leaders must often confront difficult choices and uncomfortable situations. It comes with the territory. Effective leaders don't avoid the difficult; they address it compassionately and then move on. These were basketball decisions, not personal ones. We had a culture to mend.

With the team finalized and the season opener two weeks away, it was time to get to the business of building trust amongst the players and coaches. Everyone had to trust in the vision, trust in the system and trust in one another. Without trust, there could be no change or victory.

We were building something that people thought we couldn't do—and it had nothing to do with field goal percentages, rebounds per game or any other stat we typically use to measure a team's success. This team was developing relationships and creating an atmosphere predicated on looking out for each other instead of themselves. These principles of teamwork transcend time, location, gender and profession.

I was encouraged by many of the things I saw in practice every day. I wasn't sure how many games we'd win on the scoreboard, but I was confident we'd be competitive again—which was one of our goals.

Our conference, the FCIAC, had 18 teams—which meant we'd only get to play teams once. No second-time-around adjustments. We had to be all in and be prepared to see anything and everything from our opponents. As a coaching staff, we simplified things for our players, leaving ample room to be flexible. We taught offensive and defensive principles that spelled out specific roles and rules, but we left room for players to read and react. The chaotic nature of basketball—and life—requires that.

By the season opener at home against Bridgeport Central, the guys were ready to play. They were tired of playing each other, tired of hearing my voice, ready to wear their new uniforms and Nike team shoes, and ready to compete for each other. That night—to a packed house—we didn't disappoint. For the first time in a long time, Darien beat Bridgeport Central 70-48. It was the start I was hoping for as we went into Christmas break and the Stratford Christmas Tournament.

That victory also sounded an alarm throughout the conference: the Darien game on our opponents' schedules would no longer be a guaranteed "W." It would be a fight—every time. I wondered how our team would respond to this newfound respect. It was foreign territory for a lot of these guys, and I wasn't sure how they'd handle it.

We split our games at the Stratford Christmas Tournament, and after New Year's Day we were full into our conference schedule. Going through the conference for the first time was an invaluable experience for me. It was a league with great coaches and teams like Vito Montelli at St. Joe's, Charles Bentley at Harding, Ray Barry at Norwalk, Jim Moriarty at Stamford, and Mike Walsh at Trinity Catholic. I knew the conference was going to be tough—but how tough I had no idea.

Throughout the 1994-1995 season, we found ourselves able to compete—often leading going into the fourth quarter—only to come up short time and time again. We could contend, and now we had to learn how to win, finish strong and close the deal.

While struggling to earn wins in the FCIAC, I struggled to get wins at GE Capital. Power plant workouts just wasn't a good fit for me. I hoped that over time I would develop an appreciation for the work, but I didn't. Every day, I couldn't wait to leave work for practice. That wasn't good.

Was it the work, or was it about something else? There were a lot of things to like about the job—especially the gaudy paychecks every two weeks—but did I love it? GE paid the bills, but basketball gave me the thrills. Without GE Capital, there'd be no Stamford Express or Darien. I was at a crossroads.

For many years leading up to that point, I'd advised others with the sage advice that "if you don't like doing it, you're probably not supposed to be doing it much longer. Life is too short to spend any of it in misery, especially when you can do something about it." I found myself confronted with similar circumstances.

I went to meet with my supervisor to let him know I was interested in exploring other options within GE that better suited me—hopefully something with more client interaction instead of being stuck in an office all day creating financial pricing models. But my supervisor told me he wasn't aware of other opportunities I could explore. This was GE, the largest company in the world, and there was nothing else I could do? Now what?

I decided I needed to find another job—but I knew that leaving GE Capital might have meant needing to resign as Darien's head coach, depending on where a new job might take me. I tried to focus on my job search while working on financial models, but unsuccessfully.

I left GE Capital in May of 1995 and received a generous severance package that included access to an office and phone to assist in my job search. After a rocky last chapter to the relationship, this was an amicable ending.

Later that month, I had my first job interview—for a job I never applied for. The University of the Pacific invited me out west to interview for a vacant assistant coaching position. How they knew of me remains a mystery. Their head coach, Bob Thomason, the coaching staff, the players and the university officials made me feel right at home. They were comfortable with me as a person and a coach—wheelchair and all.

When they offered me the job, I did cartwheels on the inside, unable to believe my fortune once again. I couldn't believe a Division I basketball program was interested in me. I understood how difficult it was to get into college coaching and never thought I'd ever get that opportunity. All the same, I really wasn't looking to take that route. I had just started a rebuild at Darien, and the Stamford Express was full steam ahead. I'd have to say sayonara to them both.

And then there was another caveat: The NCAA had placed a cap of a $10,000 salary for that position. When I left corporate America, I assumed I'd be taking a pay cut—but all the way down to $10,000? In Stockton, California, which had a higher cost of living, would I be able to support myself?

It couldn't be about the money. This was yet another crossroads—another question about how much I'd be willing to sacrifice to pursue my passion. By moving to California, I'd be gaining and losing so much; by staying in Connecticut I'd be gaining and losing so much. I had to let the University of the Pacific know my decision within a few days.

During that window, I received a phone call from Paul Cormier, the men's head basketball coach at Fairfield University. I had gotten to know Paul a little through his son Jon, who played on one of the Stamford Express teams.

"I heard you're in the job market," he said.

"Yes I am. I decided to leave GE Capital."

"How was California? Thomason's a good guy."

"It was great," I said. "They offered me the job. Gonna think about it over the weekend and get back to them on Monday."

"Congratulations! And actually I'm calling to see if we could meet to talk about an opportunity here at Fairfield University that just came up."

Fairfield University had recently created a position within the athletic department that Paul thought would be a good fit for me. In conjunction with the NCAA Champs Life Skills Program, Fairfield was looking for someone to build, from the ground up, a comprehensive academic support program for the athletic department's 26 varsity sports.

From a basketball perspective, this opportunity had lots of benefits. With the three to five years it would take to implement the program, I would be able to continue coaching at Darien.

And with limited summer responsibilities, I would be able to continue working basketball camps, attend basketball clinics, and travel with the Stamford Express.

Additionally, the day-to-day interactions with people I so desperately missed during my last rotation at GE Capital would not be a problem at Fairfield. I'd be back in the center of the action: hiring, training and supervising employees, and putting my MBA to good use by creating and managing tight university budgets. But the biggest draw was that it was a position that would make tangible differences in the lives of others. This was why I got involved with business and basketball to begin with.

That weekend, I met with Coach Cormier, School Vice President L. William Miles, and Athletic Director Eugene Doris. They offered me the position of Coordinator of Programs for Student Athletes.

Once again, there was one unmistakable drawback to the Fairfield job: If I accepted, it would be a 70 percent salary reduction from what I made at GE.

I had options—a decision to make. Either way, a pay cut to take.

Chapter 13: Payback

Fairfield University: Giving Back

Be the most giving person in the room, not the smartest.
Competing in giving is a race worth running.

I ACCEPTED THE POSITION AT FAIRFIELD University, and I was to begin in 60 days. One thing was for sure: no more dressing up to go to work.

I spent the rest of the 1995 summer practicing and traveling with the Stamford Express and working basketball camps at Duke University and Eastern Invitational. During the first week in August, I moved onto campus a full two weeks before the students. I traded my two-bedroom, two-bathroom high-rise apartment in downtown Stamford for a one-bedroom townhouse with upper-classmen roommates. It had shades of my Duke days, when I worked hand-in-hand with undergraduate student managers. But this time I didn't just work with them; I lived with them.

Did others question my decision? I heard it all—even from the people who previously encouraged me to follow my passions in life. They asked, "How could you give up such an opportunity? Why aren't you out in the stock market making money?"

They clearly underestimated my passions. I saw things differently. It wasn't how could I give up on the GE Capital job; it was how could I pass up on this Fairfield opportunity?

I had the chance to do what I felt I was put on this earth to do—full time. This was where my natural gifting—my vocation—resided. Money mattered, but not at the expense of fulfilling what I considered my life's purpose: inspiring others to do things they dreamed possible. I was so hungry to follow my dreams that I was willing to make that choice.

I wasn't going to be just brewing Gatorade, shagging loose balls, and doing the team's laundry anymore—though it all helped me get to where I was. Others' lives would be more directly and seriously impacted by my work. It would be a big change, and awkward at times, yet it was an essential step for me to do my job while making ends meet. I was ready.

Once I was all settled in—making sure that all my music was in the townhouse and the Smokey Joe grill was on the porch—it was time to get to work. I spent the first few days learning my way around campus, meeting key stakeholders and people in other departments who serviced the university's students. If I were to build a successful program, I couldn't do it in isolation. I took inventory of the services the university already provided students and formed partnerships with experienced student support providers who could mentor me and teach me the university's culture.

At that point, I had no office, no staff and no official name. Debbie Chappell, Dean of Freshmen, was instrumental in helping me form a winning team. My budget allowed me to hire two graduate assistants. Given that we'd be working with student athletes, hiring former student athletes with good character, competence and communication—the same qualities I looked for when hiring assistant coaches—felt necessary to meet the students at their level.

That fall, Fairfield added football to the university's varsity sports program, which increased the number of varsity student athletes in the school and increased the urgency to install support systems to monitor and assist them. Within this first year, I piloted programs focusing on time management, test preparation, peer tutoring, team study tables and goal setting. Our department programs targeted the freshman class of 2000 and relied on coaches and university staff to help identify upperclassmen who could also benefit from them.

We decided to name the program after the stag, the school's mascot: Skills to Achieve Growth and Success (S.T.A.G.S.). In conjunction with the NCAA's Champs Life Skills Program, we aspired to help student athletes develop the skills required to achieve success in the classroom, on the court or field, and in their careers.

Fairfield officials talked about breaking ground on a 51,000-square-foot facility that would cater to the academic and athletic needs of the university's student athletes. The space included a 2,000-square-foot academic support center, equipped with study carrels, group study areas and the latest technology. But for now, S.T.A.G.S. had to settle for a converted female officials' locker room in Alumni Hall.

Working in academia was quite an adjustment for me. Things took a lot longer to get done than in the corporate world. Change was annoyingly glacial. There was a committee and meeting for what seemed like everything. However, these frustrations were offset by the success stories we witnessed.

Evan Knight was a freshman football player from Massachusetts. He was a big guy who played left guard on the offensive line of the newly formed football team. Tough and competitive, Evan had everything a coach looked for on the gridiron. Off the field, Evan was one of the most compassionate student athletes I'd ever met. He looked out for and cared for others by nature, even when he found himself in his own overwhelming circumstances.

Evan entered Fairfield with a major in engineering, but he quickly found himself in an academic hole that landed him on academic probation during the first semester. According to his teachers, Evan was "lazy and disinterested" in class and didn't put enough time in to succeed. The head football coach stopped by our office to discuss Evan's academic struggles and to help piece together a plan to get him back on his feet.

We started small, concentrating on his toughest subject: math. One of my graduate assistants was a math major and started tutoring him a few times per week. When we met with Evan, he always appeared tired, which was consistent with what his teachers reported. But this felt different. It wasn't the usual head nodding off that typically accompanied tiredness. During tutoring sessions, one moment he'd be paying attention and engaged with the material only to suddenly break out into deep-sleep snoring. With a slight nudge, Evan would reawaken and refocus as if he had never fallen asleep.

This didn't just happen once. At first, we attributed Evan's fatigue to adjusting to the demands of being a college student athlete with morning workouts, afternoon practices, classes in between and late-night studying. We adjusted our schedule so we could meet with him earlier in the day instead of in the evenings. The same thing happened.

Evan never missed a tutoring session and never skipped a class or practice—despite the extra running and yelling he endured. This didn't feel like "lazy and disinterested" to me. Something wasn't right, and I wanted to figure out what it was.

I organized a meeting with the university's learning specialist. When I described what had been happening with Evan, she immediately asked if he'd ever been tested for a sleeping disorder. I didn't know and had never thought of asking him. Evan came from a rather modest background, and I doubted he would have had the resources to get tested. My assumptions were correct.

We arranged for Evan to undergo a series of tests to see if he tested positive for any identifiable sleep disorder. The results were conclusive: Evan suffered from sleep apnea. He wasn't lazy or disinterested; he had a treatable health issue. Once again, relying on the other players on the team helped us get the job done.

Evan attained the medication and equipment he needed to help diminish the side effects of sleep apnea. But I wasn't done with him; there was still the matter of overcoming his academic challenges.

Like many students, Evan entered college declaring a major that he knew little about but had a nice ring to it. Mechanical engineering passed that test, but his early struggles in math led me to believe he should consider a new path—something he was naturally good at that he could parlay into a career—something I had experience with myself.

So many people throughout my life were there for me at just the right time and place to get me to where I needed to go, and I wanted to be that person for Evan. I saw a lot of myself in him—namely, an ability to connect with and help others. For me, basketball had become my conduit; for Evan, a degree in sociology would become his springboard.

For the next three years, we worked closely with Evan and watched him chip away at his academic hurdles. He went from academic probation to graduating with his class to a career as a social worker, where he is now using his natural gifts to make others' lives better.

Evan was one of several success stories that reinforced why I left corporate America. The payback far exceeded the pay cut, since it put me in contact with people like Evan. Evan represented the "why" behind what I did. Helping others discover their purpose was evolving into my purpose.

I met many other interesting people at Fairfield, too—one of them a graduate student named MariPat, who tutored student athletes. An accomplished athlete with retired jersey numbers in volleyball, basketball, and softball, MariPat was a former Division I athlete in women's basketball. She was a person of faith who shared my passion for sports and helping people. We became close, long-term friends.

With many classes out of session during the summer, I continued to jam-pack them full of basketball. The Stamford Express was expanding and experiencing regional and national success at tournament competitions. We added Ralph Baker, Owen O'Mara, Mike Sharpe, and Guy Rancourt to our coaching staff and started attracting players as far away as New York City to join our team. Even the *New York Times* caught wind of what we were doing, and they published an article about the team and our mission of helping diverse kids on and off the floor. And then what happened next took everyone by surprise.

In the spring of 1998, longtime New York City news anchor and journalist Carole Jenkins read the *New York Times* article and contacted me. She wanted to write a documentary about the Stamford Express and me. Once I recovered from the shock of it all, I agreed to meet with Carole and her daughter, also a writer and journalist, employed by Carole Jenkins Media.

During that interview, I began to understand how my life—and more importantly, the work we were doing to impact others—was inspiring and interesting to others. I hadn't seen it that way. I was simply doing what I loved.

Soon thereafter, I signed a contract with Carol Jenkins Media for the exclusive rights to my story, granting her team access to all aspects of my life for the next few months. They got to see my work at Fairfield University and my coaching for Darien High School and the Stamford Express. It was surreal having film crews and journalists everywhere. I didn't know how it all worked, but it was fun watching it all come together. I imagined it going big—with someone like Denzel Washington playing my role. It was an exciting time.

Upon entering the 1998-1999 school year, the Office of Programs for Student-Athletes had moved into the Walsh Athletic Center, and we had accomplished our long-term goal: all 26 varsity sports athletes had access to tutoring, academic advising, career counseling, resume preparation, computer lab access, and individual and group study areas.

With the academic support program successfully in place, I desired an expanded role within the athletic department—to become an official member of its management team. In any business or team setting, one's position, pay and opportunities for promotion need to be clear. For me, the latter was not. After conversations and meetings with upper management went nowhere, I understood that my current position would be as far as I could advance within the athletic department. I liked my position and how I had reinvented myself, but I wanted more. It was time for another change of clothes.

I decided my first move would be to resign as Darien's head basketball coach at the end of the 1998-99 high school season. We didn't win as many games as I would have liked, and we had our fair share of growing pains, but we did grow. We had changed the narrative and put Darien basketball back on everyone's radar.

During my tenure at Darien, I came to appreciate the relationship between coaching and teaching. The gym was our classroom; the game, our curriculum; the scoreboard, our grade book—even if it didn't tell the full story. Basketball has the means to teach valuable lessons about life: how to find victories within scoreboard losses, how to keep going in the face of disappointment, how to be a family in good times and bad times, and the importance of teamwork and effective communication for success.

I was going to miss a lot about Darien, none more than the players and our relationships. Their will and determination to climb the mountain and fight is indelibly etched in my mind. Those players changed my life.

Knowing there were no other opportunities for me at Fairfield, I was at another fork in the road. I needed to find another job—but where? And what should I do? Did I dare give corporate America another shot? I still had the Stamford Express in the summers to satisfy some of my basketball itch, should I decide to leave the world of academia and return to business.

As I rebooted my job search and discerned my next step, another prior connection linked back to me. Greg Meuler, my high school English-teacher-turned-principal at MUHS in Milwaukee, found my phone number and contacted me. He told me Marquette High was creating two new positions—Director of Diversity and Coordinator of Academic Support Services—and immediately thought of me as a worthy candidate.

Once again, it was a job and an opportunity that I wasn't looking for. I hadn't spoken with Mr. Meuler in nearly two decades, and searching for jobs in Wisconsin was not a part of my job search strategy. However, from Duke to Fairfield, I had learned to consider every opportunity, never knowing who's been watching or where my next connection will come from.

I was going home for a few days early that summer and promised to visit Mr. Meuler to discuss this position. When I did, I learned that the opportunity was a combined role. The academic support position was more clearly defined than the diversity position; the latter sprouted from a recent and unacceptable surge in attrition rates of African-American students at Marquette High. That job would focus on recruitment and retention.

They also asked if I'd be interested in coaching the junior varsity basketball team. I really wasn't expecting that, and quite frankly, I wasn't sure I wanted to. Basically, I had been coaching high-stakes basketball for six consecutive years—winters and summers. I thought I could use a break from the game and was looking forward to some anonymity—at least for a couple of years.

Before leaving, I stopped by the Humphrey Gymnasium for old time's sake— but I wasn't prepared for rush of emotion that followed. The same exhilarating feelings I had when I visited the Fuqua School of Business and Cameron Indoor Stadium flared within me. The idea of giving back to an institution that was instrumental in shaping me into the person I became didn't just intrigue me, it felt like the right thing to do.

I left without an offer but with a promise that Mr. Meuler would take a look at the budget to see what they could offer me. I was fine with that. I still had a summer of AAU basketball ahead of me, a reboot of my job search and a documentary looming in the background. Besides, I hadn't yet resigned from Fairfield University—so if everything fell through, I still had a job I liked.

The summer didn't start off the way I hoped. Carole Jenkins Media informed me that Showtime declined the documentary in the final steps of the approval process. So much for meeting Denzel.

Additionally, I hadn't heard back from Mr. Meuler for over a month since we met. Once I did, though, it was well worth the wait. He made me an offer—a very attractive one—to come back home.

It was time. The decision was pretty easy. My assignment on the east coast was complete. I wanted to leave those places better off than when I arrived, which I believed I had.

At Fairfield, Evan was one of many who successfully developed skills to achieve growth and success. Today he is a licensed social worker in Massachusetts.

At Darien, we changed the culture and ushered in greater accountability and respect within the basketball program and around the FCIAC.

And with the Stamford Express, 60 young men over a five-year period realized their dream of playing college basketball.

I returned home in August 1999, bringing with me some great memories from my time at GE Capital, Duke University, Stamford High School, Darien High School, Fairfield University and with the Stamford Express.

Giving back has payback.

CHAPTER 14: PLEASURE

Marquette High School:
The Classroom

Do what you enjoy. Enjoy what you do.
Laugh every day. Be enthusiastic.

STRAPPED WITH STAMFORD EXPRESS debt from unfulfilled pledges—and without a place to live—I returned home feeling uneasy but optimistic. Working with students and coaching JV basketball was going to be a winning recipe for me, and the opportunity to give back to my alma mater was well worth the temporary inconveniences. Besides, Marquette High offered me temporary living on school premises until I could find and purchase a home on my own. It wasn't much different from living on campus at Fairfield. I would manage.

I'd now be working shoulder to shoulder with so many of the teachers who had been there for me in high school, and I didn't waste a chance to thank them for helping me live beyond the tragedy of October 19, 1979. I'd been living off my abilities—not my disability—and I was excited for everyone to experience that with me daily. To see so many familiar faces still there during my orientation made getting to know everyone a lot easier. Still, not everything was the same as it was when I left 18 years prior.

The fussy loading dock no longer served as my only entrance into the school. The tunnel behind the stage in the O'Rourke Auditorium no longer served as my only way to the cafeteria and Blue and Gold Room. Marquette High School now contained modern elevators and accessible restrooms. I was the school's first student in a wheelchair, but there could now be others—and there were. It wasn't perfect, but from my perspective, it was real progress. Perspective allows you to see progress—great or small—and to move forward.

The other major change was me—I had changed. I was no longer a student trying to figure it out and experience being a teenager in high school. I was an adult—the diversity director—tasked with bringing diversity awareness and support to a school that struggled to recruit, retain and improve the overall experience for students from diverse backgrounds, especially students of African descent.

Diversity is a complex, challenging and ever-changing discussion in society and at most institutions—including MUHS, a Catholic, Jesuit institution. The concept of diversity is really aimed at changing behavior, and that is not easy. Lost in the midst of political and personal agendas is the fact that diversity comes down to how we treat each other—and therein lies part of the challenge. It can't solely be about one person or one type of person. To be inclusive, it must be about others—everyone—too. It takes time, patience and empathy for everyone to witness the benefits of a diverse, inclusive community.

Another challenge is that the inability to manage a student's socialization after school hours can make respecting diversity an uphill battle for any high school. It's not uncommon for people—

especially students—to behave one way in the classroom, another way in the lunchroom, and another way out of school with family and friends.

To that end, I thought it was important to start by identifying where things had improved and to show students how to overcome injustices—not just point them out. The theory I wanted to share was that as bad as things may appear to be, they're probably better than they seem and not as bad as they could be. I wanted to change the narrative. My goal was to intentionally create and sustain an environment of mutual respect, where all feel welcome and can flourish.

With the diversity landscape expanding to include individuals from diverse sexual orientations, gender and immigration statuses, I realized I needed some help to bring my goal to fruition. I was only an expert on my experiences as an American of African descent and a wheelchair user. That focus was too narrow for this position. I needed some help. But from whom? As it often does in life, opportunity knocked in the midst of my day-to-day grind.

I was in the copy room after school one day when Jacki Black, a full-time Spanish teacher and the Latino family support liaison at the school, struck up a conversation about the upcoming National Jesuit Secondary Education Association Diversity Conference.

"I'm not going," I said bluntly.

"What do you mean you aren't going?" she said. "You're the diversity director!"

"It's not wheelchair accessible. Cynthia's going in my place."

Jacki groaned. "You're kidding, right? Hopefully this doesn't happen in future years, but if it does, I'd be willing to go in your place or help out with whatever else you need as you get resituated."

"Thanks, Jacki," I said. "I'll keep that in mind."

Jacki and I formed a partnership that proved to be very productive. She understood the culture of the school and what our boundaries were as a Catholic institution, and she was willing to work within them. She also had connections and relationships with faculty in the building who were passionate about diversity and with whom I'd had difficulty connecting. Jacki offered to help me bridge that gap.

We pooled our limited resources and unlimited ideas, which made both of us better. We didn't always agree on how to address issues, but we always agreed on why we needed to address them. I was conservative on some issues and liberal on others. Jacki didn't shy away from challenging me to think and rethink things, but she always kept it respectful. The line of communication was horizontal, never vertical.

Jacki mentored me through many of the issues that went beyond my natural inclinations and knowledge. Together, we identified strategies and created programs that would benefit the students and the entire Marquette High School community. Without her assistance, my tenure as diversity director would not have been a successful one.

With the help of the MUHS Pastoral Office, in the spring of 2012 we launched a word campaign during Lent called "Speak Life" to bring attention to destructive and harmful language and actions that we, as a school community (faculty, staff and students), wanted to eliminate from our hallways. This became one of our signature diversity efforts each year and was eventually adopted by other Jesuit high schools across the country.

"Hug Wednesdays" was an offshoot of "Speak Life." Wednesday, or "Hump Day," was known as the toughest day of the week. We felt that giving hugs to one another could be a game-changer for the ones who give and receive hugs—a simple gesture with far-reaching implications. Sometimes, it's the little things. Hug Wednesdays caught on like wildfire.

What I liked best about being the diversity director was being able to attend national student conferences and the national diversity director conferences. It was during those conferences that I sharpened my public speaking skills while sharing my thoughts on issues surrounding diversity, including how to avoid making diversity divisive.

My best work, however, was done in the classroom as an economics teacher. In 2005, the administration asked me to pinch-hit for Steve Haessler, who was taking a sabbatical to complete his doctoral dissertation. Steve was the economics department at MUHS: He taught AP Economics, Introduction to Economics and AP Statistics. I suddenly became Diversity Director, Head Varsity Basketball Coach and AP Economics teacher. I agreed to teach the classes if the coordinator for academic support position was taken off my plate—and it was.

I didn't have any formal training in education, but I had my personality and natural gift to connect with young people. I assumed a lesson plan was just like a practice plan, so I approached teaching with the same zeal in which I approached basketball.

Steve Haessler left me exams he used in prior years and at that time, and Matt Jacques from the Alumni Service Corps, who graduated from Boston College and spent a semester at the London School of Economics, taught me how to not teach economics in a finance way. It took a lot of in-game adjustments—a new pair of clothes once more—but with the help of other teachers, I'd quickly get where I needed to go.

Oftentimes, my best learning came from the students themselves.

"Hey, Coach Cooks, do you have a rubric?"

"Son, do they still make those? I haven't seen one of those in years. I wasn't very good at it—could never get all the colors to match."

The class bursts in laughter. What was so funny?

"A rubric's not a Rubik's Cube. It's a form that breaks down assignments in terms of what each section of the assignment is worth."

I still had a bit to learn, but the energy of the classroom was intoxicating.

Steve Haessler never returned to Marquette High School, so what started as a substitute-teaching role became a 12-year love affair for me. It became the reason I came to work every day. Teaching economics was new to me, but teaching was not. From coaching, I knew how to inspire and instill confidence in others. I knew how to effectively communicate my expectations and points. In basketball, my job was to prepare them for the next opponent. In the classroom, my job was to prepare them for the AP Exam in May.

I decided to take a page from my coaching playbooks to help us get there: Make practices more physically and mentally demanding than the games. Quizzes—and plenty of them—became the norm. To the chagrin of my students, I introduced the "double quiz" as a best practice. There was no rule that said I couldn't give two quizzes during the same class—nor did anyone say they had to be on current material.

My exams were no joke either. I built them in such a way that there was enough time to finish them, but with no time to waste. In order to teach my students that we never have as much time as we think we have, I asked them to complete more problems in less time than what they would have seen on the AP Exam—and we did it over and over and over again. I wasn't concerned about their grades; I was concerned about them learning and producing in the postseason: the AP Exam.

My quizzes and exams were brutal, but the end results were worth it. Not only were they ready for the AP exam in May, but along the way they learned plenty about economics and life—and had a good time doing it.

Being the diversity director helped me understand that everyone was important and had a voice to be heard. I wanted this to be true in my classes. I sought to create an environment where everyone felt comfortable being who they were and wasn't hesitant to contribute to the learning that was going on. It was an environment of respect. I always welcomed and encouraged overlapping my role as diversity director with economics teacher. Some happened on purpose; others happened by accident.

"Plaid Shirt Mondays" was established as part of our economics classes. It started out as a fun thing for my students—almost like a private club or fraternity. Eventually, though, we saw plaid shirts as a symbol of unity, diversity and teamwork—ideas consistent with the school's mission to create community. It was launched as a part of our Diversity Week celebrations, and it became a tradition that extended beyond my classes and the walls of MUHS. Alumni have continued the tradition in college and beyond.

My role as the coordinator of academic support helped me to develop differentiated teaching strategies and learning styles and to reach students who struggled in my class. Failing simply wasn't an option for my students. Figuring out how my students learned—and what they were good at—was an essential part of the job, whether it was an introductory course or an AP one.

Teaching allowed me to take diversity and life talks to whole new levels. Students coined the word "theolecon" to describe our class: I could discuss issues of race, walking privilege, economic disparity, supply and demand, STDs and, of course, faith and scripture—all through the lens of capitalism.

If there was a student who had a problem with money, profit or wealth, I gave them the option to give me their money to illustrate that I was a capitalist who didn't support the classic model of wealth redistribution. However, I did want them to understand the social responsibility of everyone looking beyond themselves in order to help others with whatever was (or wasn't) in their lunch bags.

We learned economic principles and life lessons from Forrest Gump, Charlie and the Chocolate Factory, Cool Hand Luke, A Civil Action, Princess Bride, Castaway and, of course, Tucker. It didn't stop with movies—we also made pizzas, threw tennis balls into garbage cans and learned about milking cows, all in an effort to understand the laws of scarcity, diminishing marginal returns and externalities.

Whether we realize it or not, we exercise economic principles every day. There's no such thing as a free lunch; people can't do or have everything. Limited resources force people to prioritize and place value on time and money. I leveraged economic principles to teach broader life lessons. Some of them had straightforward connections to the class: "Never pay full price for anything. Never." Others had looser connections: "Stop at the red light."

My one-liners inspired students to create the "What's Cookin' Board," a compilation of some of my quotes and sayings from classes throughout the years. Some were serious; others, downright ridiculous:

"There is such a thing as a dumb question, and that was one of them."

"Only drink 100% juice."

"Save the bones for Rufus Jones, cuz Rufus don't eat no meat."

"Keep foolin' around. You got one more time."

"The exception lands you in jail; the rule keeps you out of jail."

"Hard work doesn't pay off; it makes you tired."

"Even a fool, when he is quiet, appears to be wise."

"Stop, look and listen so you don't get run over like a cat."

"If enough people tell you that your breath stinks, you should get a mint."

"That's some stuff right there."

"If you roll around in dog poop, you're going to smell like dog poop."

"I don't need a whole lot of what I don't have."

My reputation as a tough but fair teacher grew, as did the demand for my classes. In fact, taking one of my classes was voted as one of the top ten things to do as a MUHS student before graduating. The classroom was a welcomed departure from the stresses of limited resources and addressing the problems and putting out the flames that accompanied diversity work.

The classroom was where I really wanted to be. I loved coming to class every day and was ready for more. I also loved my "other" classroom, Humphrey Gymnasium.

Chapter 15: Performance

Marquette High School Basketball:
The Road to Success

Your ability will get you there, your character will keep you there,
and it will stay with others long after you're gone.

IN ADDITION TO BEING THE DIRECTOR FOR both academics and diversity, I coached the junior varsity basketball team under Coach Kurt Soderberg. In three years' time, we managed to compile a 50-10 record. When Coach Soderberg left in 2002, I took over the varsity program. The Duke experience was amazing, but to lead my alma mater after not having the chance to represent it when I was in high school was truly a special feeling.

Unlike Darien, MUHS had a tradition steeped in winning. Expectations were high: The program's success was measured by conference and state championships. By the time I took over the reins of the program, the high school basketball landscape throughout the city and state was changing.

Back in the 1970s and '80s, Marquette High was a member of the Wisconsin Independent Schools Athletic Association (WISAA) and part of the competitive Metro Conference. We mainly competed against other local private schools in the

WISAA. Over the recent decades, however, the quality of suburban public education had drastically improved, forcing many of Milwaukee's Catholic schools to shut their doors or merge.

The WISAA joined with the Wisconsin Interscholastic Athletic Association (WIAA), thus eliminating the private school state tournament. This meant that to win conference, we'd have to get through the Greater Metro Conference—featuring perennial powerhouses like Wauwatosa East and Brookfield Central. One or two losses could cost a conference championship. We couldn't afford an off night. To get to State—and win it—we'd need to get through not just the best private schools in the area, but the best public schools, too. I was eager for the challenge. It was time to put some numbers on the gym wall.

First, I had to assemble a coaching staff with knowledge and experience that rivaled any staff in the state. Percy Eddie and Mark Briggs joined me on the sidelines. Both were products of the City Conference, and their collegiate and professional experiences gave them instant credibility with the players.

Percy, a former NBA player and Kansas State alumnus, played the role of "good cop" on the team. His 6'8" frame was intimidating enough that he only had to give a look if guys were out of line. Mark played professionally overseas and was on the only UW-Milwaukee basketball team to beat UW-Madison. He excelled as a teacher of the game, whether it was offense, defense or communication—the three systems we taught. At 6'6" and with a silky-smooth jump shot, Mark was the undisputed and undefeated champion of the game H-O-R-S-E. One would think the players would eventually give up, but they tried to challenge his title for years.

Performance

Like at Darien and with the Stamford Express, I wanted us to work hard and play hard. Our practices were high level all the time. We didn't have a lot of rules, but the ones we had we valued and enforced: be early, work hard, be a good teammate and no cussing. This applied to our coaches as well.

John Willkom, a Marquette University student and former walk-on, was assisting us and used profanity during a practice one day. To the players' delight, he had to run 17s while Coach Briggs played the infamous African drum. "The Drum" regularly provided the beat for our international trips, but it wasn't the only non-basketball sound that often echoed through the gymnasium.

Tobymac, G.R.I.T.S, Mary Mary, Kirk Franklin, and many others filled the air at practices and were part of our pregame warm-up CD. Faith and music were important to me as a student at MUHS, and they stayed important to me as a coach. Listening to Contemporary Christian/Rap music also eliminated any concerns about finding "edited" or "clean" versions of songs. It aligned well with the school's overall mission.

During the dog-days of the season, I hosted an annual Super Bowl watch-party that was the envy of the school and a highlight of our season. With the game on in two rooms, the team gathered by 4:32 p.m. exactly for a few hours of fellowship and food on Super Bowl Sunday. Lots of food: La Nova Wings shipped in from Buffalo, Coach Glass's gumbo, Mrs. Foley's lemon meringue pie, Mrs. Beres' éclair ring, and everything in between.

I inherited some really good players, many of whom I coached on the JV squads, and we experienced success right away. But our playoff sectional—often called the "mini-state tournament"—was absolutely brutal. It was common to go up against three to five of the top ten teams in the state for sectionals.

The second round of the 2004 sectional playoffs was one of those situations. We were up against Wauwatosa East for the third time that season. Going into that game, "Tosa East" was ranked second in the state, and we were third (having lost to them twice earlier in the year). In front of a packed house at Tosa East, the crowd was treated to an intense, back-and-forth game decided in the last two minutes of the fourth quarter: Marquette 59, Tosa East 50. The difference this time was clear: The players bought in the strategy of relentlessly using our size advantage to score inside, get them in foul trouble, and knock down some free throws.

Our reward for winning was a date against Rufus King, the number one team in the state. The game was held at Wisconsin Lutheran on a Friday night—also the final day of MUHS' two-week long Senior Shared Life Project in which seniors served in the Milwaukee community instead of attending regular classes. From tip-off to the final buzzer, Rufus King—the eventual State Champions—controlled the game. Our guys gave it all they had, but they came up short that day. The team finished with a 20-3 record, second in the Greater Metro Conference.

Over the years, there was a common theme that developed. Schools from the City Conference, with teams that were more athletic than we were (especially on the perimeter), eliminated us from the postseason. As competitive as our conference was, we played a brand of basketball that didn't prepare us well for what we inevitably faced in the postseason.

We needed to try something different to give us a better run at State. The first thing we did was beef up our non-conference schedule. Just like in A.P. Economics, I made our schedule as difficult as possible in order to prepare us for the final test.

We scheduled games against athletic foes that could simulate what we'd see in the postseason. We regularly crossed the Wisconsin border for games against Brebeuf Jesuit in Indianapolis and Proviso East High School in Chicago, and we entered tournaments like the WBY Shootout, NY2LA Tournament and the Brandon Jennings Under Armor Tournament. These games often cost us from a win-loss perspective, but they made us more battle-tested for the regional and state tournaments.

The second move we made was hiring Neil O'Connell. "Coach O.C." came from Adams-Friendship High School, an extremely successful program with multiple state tournament appearances. My greatest success as a basketball head coach occurred when I finally listened to Coach O.C. and installed the 1-3-1 zone he used so successfully at Adams-Friendship.

I had always been a man-to-man defensive coach and was uncomfortable teaching zone defense. Instead, I wanted us to return to the glory days of my youth in the 1980s by using the schemes and strategies that made us successful then. But with the evolution of both the players and the game in the 2000s, we had a hard time defending the athletic wing perimeter players in the sectional tournament and beyond. The 1-3-1 better suited our personnel and gave us a better chance of being successful in the postseason. My pride and ignorance, a lethal combination, kept me resistant to change. It took Neil a few years to convince me, but once he did and I saw the results, I wished I had listened to him sooner.

In our 2007-2008 injury-plagued season, we first implemented the 1-3-1 into our program. It was the following season when we began to see just how effective it could be for us. The team bounced back from a 7-14 record in 2007-2008 to an 18-3-1 mark the following year. This included a 50-50 tie resulting from a leaking roof in Indiana, a signature win against Proviso East (Illinois) 61-37, and a clinching of the Greater Metro Championship in Humphrey Gymnasium against Tosa East. It was one of the deepest and most talented teams I had ever coached at MUHS. Great leaders emerged from that team, including Mike Hoffman, "Big Shot" Sam Beres and GMC Player of the Year "G-Money" Garrett Maloney.

Another highlight in 2007 was marrying my friend MariPat, who I had remained close with over the years and miles. Her dedication to helping others was admirable and appealing, as was her love for the game of basketball. She had become a math teacher who stayed active in sports as a varsity girls' high school basketball assistant coach. We made a good team—and still do.

With most of the 2008-2009 team returning the following year after losing to Tosa East in the playoffs, expectations were high. Losing to a team that they beat at the end of the regular season fueled their motivation in the off-season. Unfortunately, we started the season slow. We went 3-5 in the first eight games, with our fifth loss coming after squandering a 20-point second half lead to upstart Germantown High School.

With the talent and experience on the team, there was no reason "on paper" that our record should be where it was. But like I used to say, paper don't play—players do. It was time for us to have a team meeting to see if we could get to the bottom of our underperformance.

I opened the meeting with this question: "What is it that you guys need from me?"

Mark Haas, a senior captain and fierce competitor with a championship pedigree as a member of the storied MUHS soccer program, spoke up first. "We need you to coach us."

That wasn't the response I expected, but that's the benefit of creating a culture where honest communication and open dialogue are encouraged. We were a veteran team, and I thought that meant I could be a bit more hands-off than previous, less experienced teams. Surely they'd be able to figure things out on their own more during games. Besides, we worked really hard in practice to get them prepared. What was he actually asking me to do?

The game of basketball is controlled chaos. It forces you to be quick on your feet—literally and figuratively—if you're going to compete and win. The best coaches and leaders are able to interpret the chaos and provide instruction, instill confidence and show support to the players in order to execute the game plan at a high level.

Thanks to Mark, who fearlessly spoke up, I realized I needed to use my timeouts more strategically and look for moments in the games to settle and refocus the team when the controlled chaos wavered on the brink of disorder. Part of communication is listening. Learning to listen—and listening to learn—breeds leaders who are team players. Listening to your players and staff serves as an incubator for new ideas and creative solutions. I learned that principle with Coach O.C.'s 1-3-1 zone, and I was learning it again.

Every team, regardless of talent or experience, needs to be coached. This talented, veteran team was no exception.

After that game-changing team meeting, we played the remainder of the season to a 16-4 record, passing sectionals, passing regionals, and making it to the State Tournament for the first time since joining the WIAA. What made this journey so special was the route we had to take. We were a #7 seed in our sectional and defeated the City Conference schools who had repeatedly eliminated us in the past:

Marquette 56, Milwaukee Bay View 44.
Marquette 54, Milwaukee Riverside 43.
Marquette 53, Milwaukee Washington 43.
Marquette 80, Milwaukee King 47.
Marquette 48, Milwaukee Hamilton 43.

This team changed the way the game was played in our conference and in southeastern Wisconsin. The 1-3-1 zone was no longer solely for teams from the northern parts of the state. We held offensively explosive teams to the 40s, thanks to our 2-2-1 full court zone press and our 1-3-1 half court zone. That was our system. But getting to the championship game and winning it was our team goal. We were now just one step away. Arrowhead High School was our final opponent, and we had payback on our minds from a late-season 14-point loss to them at home.

The atmosphere at the Kohl Center in Madison, Wisconsin was electric. It was akin to what Cameron Indoor Stadium was like on game day. Down ten points with three minutes to go, we clawed back—only to lose at the buzzer on a bank-shot three from the top of the key. Marquette 58, Arrowhead 60. A defensive breakdown, an error in communication, cost us on that final play.

The emotional roller coaster of that game's final moments, when we took the lead but then lost the game, exemplified "the thrill of victory and agony of defeat." It had everything you could ever want in a basketball game. I was so proud of what that team accomplished then, and I'm still proud today.

That team, the class of 2011, was a special one—recording a 37-5 conference record and the school's first trip to the WIAA State Tournament. Replacing that class would prove difficult over the next couple of years, but looking down the road, I was confident there'd be another chance on the horizon to return to Madison.

Chapter 16: Promotion

Marquette High School Basketball:
Getting Fired

*It is impossible to live without failing at something,
so don't let that stop you from getting to your destiny.
Embrace it, learn from it and get back in the line.*

IT WAS THE FIRST DAY OF SPRING BREAK on Wednesday, March 27, 2013. I wanted to wrap up a few things before heading out to San Diego for vacation with my wife. I decided to see if the athletic director was in the building so we could put a bow on the 2012-2013 season and plan for the next one—my 12th as head coach. He was, and we met in my office.

After the dynamite graduating class of 2011, we'd had a few sub-par seasons. We finished seven games under 500 in 2011-2012 before rebounding in 2012-2013 to one game over 500. We were excited about the talent at the JV and freshman levels. As a program, we decided not to move up any of the players to varsity so they could build chemistry and confidence together.

Primed for 2013-2014 success, we reviewed the past season's performance and discussed the next season's schedule, strategy and expectations. We wrestled with launching a junior Hilltopper feeder program, and we noted staff and equipment needs. About 45 minutes into our meeting, I thought we were heading toward the end of our discussion. Then things took an unexpected turn.

"David, I need to talk to you about one more thing. It's a difficult thing."

What could be left to talk about? I thought. "Okay, what's up?"

"We need to go in another direction," the athletic director said.

"No problem. Where are we going?"

Loud silence. The athletic director seemed uncomfortable and put his head down.

"We are going in another direction in terms of the basketball program."

"Are you firing me?"

"We decided to go in another direction. Your contract will not be renewed."

"So you are firing me. This is coming out of left field. Can you tell me why?"

What had I done—or not done? Was it winning? A donor? Something else? There were no improvement plans, no documentation shared with me, no prior discussions about my performance. This felt so far out of left field that I felt I deserved an explanation so I wouldn't make the same mistakes again if I had another opportunity to coach.

I couldn't get a clear answer from the athletic director. Perhaps he was just the messenger, but that's mere speculation. There were no other administrators in the building I could talk to, either, with it being the first day of break. Regardless, it was over. Abruptly.

I was fired as the Marquette High School basketball coach.

Before leaving my office, I called my wife to inform her of the school's decision. Our vacation would have a different feel. In the parking lot, I ran into Anthony Houston, one of the greatest to ever wear an MUHS uniform. I told him what had happened. At first he thought I was messing with him—but once he recognized my sincerity, he stood with me in disbelief, shaking his head.

Later that evening, I contacted my coaching staff—freshman through varsity—to thank them for their service and commitment over the years and to tell them I've been fired. I wanted to give them as much time as possible to look for other coaching opportunities if that's what they were looking to do.

The next day, I met with the school principal in hopes of getting some answers—about their decision, about the process, and about my role as economics teacher and diversity director. The principal referred all basketball-related questions back to the athletic director; however, he said I'd resume teaching economics and he was excited that now I'd be able to spend more time on diversity.

I left the principal's office about the same way I came in: confused and still searching for an explanation. I had lost trust in and respect for the school's leadership. I felt angry and betrayed. Who could I trust? How could I make this work?

I had ten days to process all of this before returning to school. It was the first time I'd ever been fired, been told I couldn't do something I wanted to do, been undressed like that. But overcoming obstacles was in my DNA.

During my decades of coaching experience, I preached how important it is to move on to the next play. You can't dwell on one bad play because it compounds into two, then three bad plays, and then you really cost yourself and your team. It was my turn to go on to the next play. Regardless of the route or the amount of time it took, I was confident I'd come out on the other side with a win. One day at a time, one moment at a time, one footprint at a time—because that's all I could do.

I wasn't as bad as rejection was saying I was, but I probably wasn't as great as I thought I was, either. All the same, my character and integrity were still intact. I had more to give. Rejection provided me the opportunity to reflect, regroup and re-launch.

Reflect. What things did I do well? If I could do things differently, what would they be? What mistakes have I made? What could I do moving forward to better utilize my skill set?

The more I reflected, the more I realized I had a lot to be thankful for. 14 years ago, Marquette High School had given me this opportunity to be part of the basketball program and be on a powerful and public stage. I was grateful for all the teams and players, and I was grateful for all the games—over 300 in total. With a varsity record of 155-92-1, Conference Championships, exciting State Tournament runs and a state Coach of the Year award in 2010, I took a step back from the rejection and observed all I had to be proud of. While looking through newspaper articles, letters and other memorabilia, I came across an email that encouraged me.

PROMOTION

From: Jeff Winkler
Sent: Monday, April 05, 2010
To: Sazama, Fr. Warren
Subject: Marquette University High School Should Be Proud

Reverend Warren Sazama,

I am writing to let you know of a great display of encouragement, positive thinking and respect that Mr. David Cooks displayed at the WIAA State Tournament. I had the pleasure of being in the first row of the crowd, directly behind the MUHS team, when they played Milwaukee Hamilton. I always enjoy a good high school basketball game, but this one will be in my memory forever. I had the distinct pleasure of watching Mr. David Cooks coach those young men with positive comments and a level of respect that I have never observed at a high school game. I came home that night and checked to see if there was a website I could go to learn more about your school and your basketball coach.

It was quite a surprise for me to see that one of Mr. Cooks' coaching highlights was working for Coach K at Duke University. I guess this shouldn't have been a surprise —I always knew that Coach K was a very classy and respected coach—and I now have another coach that I will include on my list of "Coaches with Class."

I should have mentioned that my 20-year-old son was sitting next to me during the entire game, and we both mentioned how refreshing it was to see a coach treating kids with respect and positive thinking and displaying a level of confidence that spread through all the players on the team.

Congratulations on a very successful basketball season— but even more important are the lessons that Mr. David Cooks has taught those boys about teamwork, confidence and respect.

I sure hope to see Coach Cooks at the State tournament next year!
Sincerely,
Jeff Winkler
(Just a basketball fan from Deerfield, WI)

Gratitude and anger can't coexist. It's not possible to be thankful for everything that happens, but there's always room for thanks in everything that happens. The more I focused on the positives, the less I dwelled on what I could no longer control.

Regroup. Is my head on straight again? Have I thought this through enough? Am I ready to make a rational decision? What are my short and long term goals? What are my new desired outcomes?

You can't drive a car by looking in the rear-view mirror. It's good to glance in it to see where you've been and what might appear, but you need to face forward and think forward in order to move forward safely.

I was down, but not out. I was redirected, but not redefined. In the midst of embarrassment and hurt, it was important for me to cheer for myself now, to confirm that I wasn't a good coach, but a great one who did things the right way. I did everything with integrity and with the best interest of the players and school in mind and at heart. I didn't always get it right, but I was committed to trying to get it right.

I would need to rebrand and reinvest in myself as part of this process, and I was willing to do whatever it would take. I was ready to explore new opportunities and continue being part of the game I loved so much. Staying on the sidelines was not an option. Coaching was what I loved doing, and I still had more to give. But how could I do this and still maintain a full-time teaching job?

Re-launch. What is it that I want to do? Where do I want to go? What's my next step?

Not long after getting fired, I received a phone call from Wisconsin Hall of Fame radio announcer, host of The Varsity Blitz, and my good friend Mike McGivern. He didn't ask what happened or how I was feeling. He wanted to know what was next. What was the next play?

Too often, our friends allow us to remain too long in a place of pain instead of encouraging us to move on and find the next opportunity as part of the healing process. The Marquette High School coaching door had closed, but Mike reminded me that doors open, too—even during times of pain. I was now ready to move forward and replace my terminated extra-curricular activity with something else, where I could continue impacting lives through the great game of basketball.

Mike suggested that I give Shawn Cassidy, the men's head basketball coach at Concordia University, a call. Mike thought recruiting and assistant coaching would be a perfect fit. At the college level, I'd get a chance to do something I was gifted to do by building relationships with players and families and teaching the game to college athletes. Additionally, Concordia is a faith-based institution, and Mike knew that would appeal to me and provide another platform to share my faith with others.

Coach Cassidy agreed to meet with me. This time, it only took one phone call to win a meeting. I had come a long way in 20 years. Coach Cassidy had just lost one of his assistant coaches and was very interested in me joining the program. For three hours, we talked about basketball, mission, accessible travel arrangements and our past. He was familiar with me because Marquette High participated in the annual WBY Shootout hosted by Concordia University during the Christmas holiday season.

Coach Cassidy offered me the position. Without my experience head coaching at Marquette High, this wouldn't have been possible. I'd been promoted. I was now an assistant college coach at Concordia. A successful re-launch.

Losing the MUHS basketball job did not distract or diminish the effectiveness of my day job. In fact, it may have made it even more clear that impacting lives was not restricted to the hardwood. Gifts are not often isolated to one environment. I loved the classroom. The students and my economics classes continued to be the reason I'd get up every morning for work.

The summer of 2013 was great. I worked with the Concordia basketball coaches on ball screen defense and the dribble drive offense. I got my first taste of recruiting high school athletes. I built up a network by connecting and reconnecting with other high school and college coaches on the recruiting circuit. I fell in love again with the game I adored as a young boy, playing with my friends until the street lights turned on.

When I returned to MUHS to start my 15th year after an eventful summer, the school year started the same way the last one had ended—with me in shock and disappointment. One of my classes, Introduction to Economics, had been given to another teacher. It was déjà vu having something I was good at and really enjoyed taken away without any communication. There was nothing I could do about the change, but I was responsible for how I responded. I was grateful for what I could still contribute and more determined than ever to make the classes I still had the best ever. How the 2013-2014 school year began would not be an indication of what the remainder of the school year would be like.

During the previous couple of years, Guy Rancourt had been in contact with me about joining him and the USA East Coast

Basketball team for an international summer experience in Europe. But with my summer responsibilities as a head coach, it hadn't been possible before. He contacted me again in the fall of 2013 to see if I'd be interested and able to join him on his next overseas trip in 2014. He wanted to pay me back for helping him when he needed it most some 20 years ago.

I first met Guy when he recently graduated from college and I lived in Connecticut and was coaching the Stamford Express. Guy was from New York City and a "city guy"—opinionated, enthusiastic and very energetic. He was chasing his dream of becoming a college basketball coach when he reached out to me for my help with the Express. He had previously worked as an assistant coach at Trumbull High School, a school in the FCIAC, and he came highly recommended. I welcomed him into our program and made sure we did everything we could to help him fulfill his dream.

After working with us for a few years, Guy landed his first coaching job at John Jay College in New York City. He was named Coach of the Year in his first season and never looked back. He spent time at Stony Brook University and Florida State University before settling in at Lycoming College in Pennsylvania, where he regularly had them nationally ranked.

During his summers, Guy had been taking Division I college all-star teams to Europe to play basketball and offer players a culturally immersive experience. Guy offered me a chance to help coach one of these squads with him and Frank Martin, South Carolina men's basketball head coach, during the summer of 2014.

Without the responsibilities of being a head coach and with more flexibility in my summer schedule, I eagerly accepted Guy's offer. Players from Lycoming, Baruch, Syracuse, Arkansas, Iowa, South Carolina and Kansas would make up this team's roster. From high school to college to USA East Coast basketball, I considered it another promotion and a chance to grow as a coach and person—and to represent my country abroad was another honor for me.

In March of 2014, about one year after being fired, the president and athletic director came to see me separately about having an "Evening of Gratitude" at Marquette High School to honor me for the years I served as the varsity basketball head coach. I wasn't interested in having the event and reopening old wounds. Besides, the school was in the midst of their second head varsity basketball coaching search in a year. It just seemed a little awkward to me. Nonetheless, they persisted and I eventually agreed. The event would be held later that year, in June, and I offered to help in any way I could to make it a success.

Later that spring, the class of 2014 voted me to be the faculty speaker at their commencement ceremony. I had spoken at assemblies, retreats and other school programs, but to have the chance to speak to the faculty, students, and parents at my alma mater was a unique privilege—one greater than coaching basketball. After a tumultuous last year and a half, it felt extra-vindicating to know that students still believed in me and wanted to hear what I had to say—and not only the students in my class. I'd also be the first African-American faculty member to speak at an MUHS commencement ceremony.

Promotion

Sunday, May 25, 2014 had finally arrived. Immediately, my mind went back to my graduation ceremony in 1982 when Jim Van Eerden pushed me up the ramp and onto the stage in Humphrey Gymnasium. I thought about how I never got to play basketball in front of a packed house, but that I had enjoyed 14 years of coaching here. I thought about that moment a little over a year before, when I had gathered my players in this gymnasium and told them I'd no longer be their coach. Humphrey Gymnasium was a special place, and it would be the final commencement ceremony ever to be held there. What a beautifully complicated history it had for me, and what an honor it was to bid it, and the class of 2014, farewell.

That day, when they introduced me and called my name to address the class of 2014, I rolled myself up the ramp and onto the stage, with my briefcase on my lap and a bottle of cranberry juice tucked away in the podium. And then I began. I spoke about the number 14 and how it represents good and charity—everything the class of 2014 represents. I spoke about servant leadership—making other people's lives better. And I spoke about how regardless of our flaws, we are all qualified to make the lives of others better. Here's the ending to my address:

"Live life with integrity. The pages of the next chapter in your lives are empty. Much of what will be written about you will be based off the choices you make during this portion of your journey. There's nothing wrong with trying to get it right every time. Just remember, Class of 2014, you—yes you—are equipped to represent the good and charitable.

Every ending promises a beginning. Now is such a time. Go now and may passion inspire you. May injustice trouble you and cause you to respond. May friendship nourish you. May you get it right more than you get it wrong. May you laugh often. May peace surround you. May love permeate you. May gratitude overwhelm you.

And as you go, may you find the right questions to ask, may you give more than you have received, and may you know the depth of your knowledge and of your compassion—now, and in the days to come. Live simply. Act justly. Speak honestly. May the love of God that overcomes all differences, that heals all wounds, that puts to flight all fears, that reconciles all who are separated, be in you and among you now and always.

I pray the blessing of the Lord, which makes one wealthy in all areas of one's life and add no sorrow, be upon you and in you. Amen. Amen. Amen."

And with those parting words, the school year had officially ended. But there was one more school-related activity left: The Evening of Gratitude in June.

The parents did a great job of getting the word out as best they could. There was some mix-up that resulted in the event not being advertised on social media—but former players, administrators, families, coaches and coaches from other Milwaukee schools showed up and made the event a stunning success. There was an open mic that evening, and the stories and memories people shared were outstanding. I was hoping to hear from the administration that evening, but unfortunately, it didn't happen.

The night capped off with a DVD presentation sent by Coach K, followed by the announcement that I'd be representing the United States with USA East Coast Basketball in August. A couple of days later, I received a check in the mail from the parents of former players, covering all my travel expenses with USA East Coast Basketball as a "token of their appreciation." Again, I thought how none of this would have been possible without MUHS giving me a chance. I was, and still am, grateful.

Before leaving for Europe, two co-workers and I met with the principal to discuss diversity from an employee's point of view. We sought clarity on the school's mission and direction. At the end, I expressed my desire to have an expanded role in the classroom and to eventually be phased out of the diversity director role. I had served in that capacity for 15 years and was experiencing burnout. The average shelf life for diversity directors in Jesuit high schools is about four years.

As was the case at GE Capital and Fairfield University, I looked to maintain my job but with different responsibilities. Like at those other places, the response I heard was "no." My co-workers looked at me, and I at them. I didn't consider my request beyond the realm of consideration or possibility. I felt a similar shock as when my coaching contract wasn't renewed and when my economics class was taken away. I would deal with this after I returned from my travels.

Chapter 17: Prayer

Faith Matters

Hope drives us from despair to achievement.
Against all odds, we have to believe; we have to hope when there is no hope, because if we don't, we'll be overcome by our circumstances.

THE ABILITY TO BELIEVE MIGHT BE THE single greatest gift bestowed upon humankind. Who and what you believe in affects how you live and the decisions you make.

My parents modeled for me what it means to be a Christian. It was their consistent and persistent faith that led me to want to serve the same God they served. Interestingly, neither came from a church or religious background, but they lived a pretty clean life: no drinking, no smoking, no cussing, no carousing. When they went out, it was strictly for birthdays and anniversaries, and they were very selective about where they'd go in the city.

My mom was primarily a homemaker who frequently worked part-time nights as a nurse's aide. The youngest of 18 children, she left Mississippi at the age of 17 with 50 dollars and a bus ticket, and she headed due north in search of work and a way to reunite with some of her brothers and sisters.

After settling in Milwaukee with her five sisters, my mom studied nursing at the University of Wisconsin-Milwaukee.

She struggled in math, and one of her classmates knew of a young man who might be able to help. That man became her tutor, her friend, her boyfriend, her husband and, eventually, my father.

Besides being a math whiz, my dad worked as an instrument technician for the City of Milwaukee Water Department. At night, he performed as an entertainer and singer. His baritone voice would carry rooms as he sang Broadway hits and jazz classics on the circuit in downtown Milwaukee.

In the middle of the 1970s, my dad began to make a name for himself as a singer. He performed regularly at Milwaukee's Pfister Hotel, sharing the stage with jazz legends like the late-great Al Jarreau. His act also went national. I remember staying up late to watch him perform on the Joan Rivers Show on our 13-inch black-and-white TV with rabbit ears and an antenna. It was pretty cool to watch my dad on TV as a ten-year-old.

Despite his growing reputation within the industry, the traps that often accompany the entertainment world weren't attractive to my dad. He was a family man who absolutely adored his wife. Success and fame meant nothing compared to his love for my mom.

Later that year, my dad got an even bigger break: He landed a two-week engagement in the Crown Room of Milwaukee's Pfister Hotel, the only night spot that regularly employed nationally known entertainers. Right before he began his two-week stint, however, something happened that changed my entire family's lives.

My brother and I were upstairs in bed when we heard my dad's voice booming through the heating vent. We were pretty used to this, often hearing him practice at night. What was strange, though, was that we couldn't make out a word he was singing. What was going on?

The next morning, Dad announced to the family that he had surrendered his life to Christ. The voices we heard through heating vent belonged to my father, but he was speaking in tongues, having experienced a baptism in the Holy Spirit.

A what? I remember thinking. I had no idea what he was talking about.

That week, my dad informed his band and agent that he would no longer perform with them after fulfilling his two-week contract with the Crown Room. He wanted to use his musical gifts another way—to bring glory and honor to Christ.

Privately, I questioned the validity of his conversion. *This is a phase*, I told myself. Maybe he'd join a church, become a cantor, join a choir—no big deal. Like all phases, this, too, will pass. You couldn't possibly give all this up for God. Boy, was I wrong.

Church took on a new meaning. Family took on a new meaning. The Bible took on a new meaning. II Corinthians 5:17 became his new anthem: "Therefore, if anyone is in Christ, the new creation has come: The old has gone, the new is here!" I was able to see the transformative power of Jesus Christ up close and personal. My dad's relationship with God was now a personal one that permeated every area of his life. Everything he did, everything he said, everything he thought, he now did to glorify God.

Several years later, I found out my mom also had a spiritual experience—two months prior to Dad's Damascus Road-like conversion. Hers was a simple prayer of surrender in her bed, acknowledging her need for a Savior.

My parents experienced a change of clothes and were now on their way to fulfilling their God-designed purpose as parents and as husband and wife. More important than the clothes they shed were the clothes they put on—especially for my dad.

He traded in his microphone from the nightclubs to go minister through song at prisons, hospitals, nursing homes, prayer meetings and churches—Catholic and Protestant, black and white, male and female, urban and rural. Their new lives reflected diversity in its simplest form: the willingness to interact and build relationships with people from different walks of life. I saw them repeatedly love and welcome people into their lives who, based upon the Jim Crow South, were "supposed" to shun and be skeptical of as African-Americans. More than anything I saw, this was proof to me—at a very early age—that their faith was real, and so was Jesus.

There were no addictions, vices or desperate circumstances that led my parents to seek Christ and do His will. Their conversions didn't happen in a confessional, a revival, a retreat or at a Sunday morning service. God met them right where they were in our home. And they were transformed.

My parents never forced me to accept or reject Christ into my heart and life. They encouraged me, supported me, reassured me that "to all who did receive him, to those who believed in His name, he gave the right to become children of God," (John 1:12); but ultimately, I was responsible for figuring out if I wanted to make Christ the focal point of my life, too. They couldn't do that for me. As they said, "God doesn't have grandchildren, only children."

I had witnessed Christ's power and salvation work through my parents and saw how their lives were transformed. I had witnessed countless miracles of healing—from drug addicts to blind and deaf individuals. I had witnessed Christ working through people with no physical, mental or emotional challenges whatsoever, yet Christ made their lives more complete, too. I came to understand that the greatest miracle isn't a physical one, but a spiritual one. Salvation—the ability for anyone to enter into a relationship with Christ—changed everyone who opened their hearts from the inside-out.

It wasn't a matter of if or why I should enter into such a relationship; it was why wouldn't I want to dedicate my life to Him?

At the age of 13, after a Friday-night youth service at New Jerusalem Temple Church, I surrendered my life to Christ. No lightning. No thunder. No earthquake. No major lifestyle changes. Just a sense of peace. Something on the inside had changed: Christ now lived within me. From that day forward, whatever happened, I wanted my life and heart in His hands. It was the first time in my life that I was all in—and I was still a walking teenager at the time.

I had no idea that two years later my faith in God and His Word would be tested in the form of an aneurysm. Was I going to divorce from Him? Was I now going to serve Him just because I needed a miracle?

It's always easier to believe for others' miracles or to tell them what to believe when they're facing adversity. But when it's you facing a seemingly insurmountable situation, it's not so easy. Because of all that I'd seen and heard, I knew that there was nothing too difficult for God to handle—including my questions and disappointment.

As I lay in bed that first night in St. Michael's Hospital, I made a pact with myself and chose to dictate my circumstances and to be victorious—instead of having the circumstances dictate me. I vowed to live in each moment and find victories in each moment. With the same unconditional commitment I made when I allowed Christ into my heart and life, I committed to my cause and to moving forward with character, integrity and consistency.

That wasn't to say that my circumstances didn't exist. I still had six months of rehabilitation in front of me. I still had as much of an unknown present as an unknowable future. But my aneurysm didn't have the right to rule the rest of my life. I couldn't be riddled in fear and anger and "what if's" to the point that I'd stop living.

My aneurysm wasn't some crude punishment; however, it would impact the road I'd need to take to achieve my purpose in life. I had faith in God's ability to perform, and I needed faith in his ability to help me endure and overcome.

The Word of God is filled with people who faced difficulties and challenges and emerged victorious, fulfilling their destinies and purposes. I used it as a source of encouragement and inspiration. Surrendering my life to Christ didn't make me immune to life's problems, but it did guarantee an abundant, full life and an eventual victorious ending.

My life has been full of challenges, but loaded with victories. God has graced me with making the difficult look easy; the uncomfortable, comfortable; the unbelievable, believable. His strength continues to be made perfect in my weakness. On October 19, 1979, I expected to walk again someday. My expectation is still the same today. God's Promises are "Yes" and "Amen!" Christ in me, the Hope of glory!

Jesse Cooks transitioned to heaven in 2012, and his zeal for God never diminished over the years—even up to his death. His legacy of touching lives for the Kingdom of God is alive and well.

My dad taught me so many things, like fishing, riding a bicycle, cutting the grass, treating people with respect and handling finances. But the greatest things he taught me were spiritual—to pray, to study God's Word, and to uncompromisingly live for God. What you believe does matter, and so does the road you take.

At a fork in the road once again, I believed that after 17 years, my assignment at Marquette High School might be complete. I didn't know exactly what would be next, but I knew that "making other people's lives better" would be at the core of my next assignment. God's got me.

Faith to believe. Faith to endure. Faith to overcome.

Chapter 18: Purpose

Making Other People's Lives Better

The journey to discovering your purpose and reaching your destiny will include tough times and difficult situations.
Keep moving forward, regardless of how small the move.
You are fully equipped to run YOUR race. Never retreat. Never quit.

THE TRIP TO EUROPE COULDN'T HAVE COME at a better time. I needed to get away from it all in order to process things. Consider my next move. The "next play." To un-focus in order to refocus.

Traveling to Estonia and Finland with USA East Coast Basketball was fantastic and exceeded my expectations. I learned from some of the best college basketball minds the game offered, and I got to coach some of the best young athletes in the world. Traveling internationally with someone in a wheelchair can be complicated, but despite some challenges identifying accessible housing and transportation, Guy didn't let that stop him. I'll never forget that. It was a special way to celebrate my 50th birthday.

When I returned to the States, the dilemma I left behind still remained. I always assumed I would retire from Marquette High School, but I decided that the 2015-2016 school year would be my last as a member of their faculty. After 17 years of growth and discovery, it was time for me to venture on to the next phase of my journey. Thankfully, I found that this wasn't a difficult decision for me anymore; it was the right decision.

Through coaching, teaching and directing diversity, MUHS helped nourish and develop my gifts. Though I was passionate about coaching and teaching, my purpose was to positively impact lives. It was because of MUHS that I knew I could now leave feeling prepared for my next assignment—wherever it was and whatever I would do. My gift to reach people most certainly stretched beyond the halls of MUHS.

Returning to corporate America was a distinct possibility. There were aspects of it that I missed in academia, especially the deal making and strategic planning. As a first step in this next phase, I met with several CEOs and business leaders in the Milwaukee area. I wanted to explore the marketplace to see what opportunities were out there that matched my educational background and professional experience.

To assist in the process, I worked with a manager of global talent acquisition at a Fortune 500 company. As we searched for a position to match my skill set, he said something I had never heard from a human resource manager before:

"David, my job is to put you in a position to do what it is that you were born to do and maximize your gifts and talents. Let's figure out what that is."

What I was born to do? What is my mission in life?

Shortly after that meeting, another Fortune 500 company in Milwaukee contacted me, and I interviewed for a director position in charge of global pricing for one of their divisions. I was interviewed by the person vacating the position for another within the firm, and he asked me a timely and important question:

"Why would you want to come and do this when what you are doing is so honorable and noble? For the most part, anyone can do what I do; but not everyone can do what you do."

I couldn't answer him. The more I reflected, the more I grew convinced that corporate America wouldn't fulfill my mission. Despite that, I continued interviewing in big business and was offered comfortable six-figure salaries. I justified considering these positions because I thought the money would help me fulfill my purpose. Besides, I had willingly made significant financial sacrifices for the past 20 years.

Then I thought of my dad. He maximized his natural gifts and talents for performing and found a way to match it with his purpose. He willingly sacrificed a life many performers dreamed of, and it transformed his life. What did I need to do?

Transition requires faith. I didn't know where I was going to land, but what I was going to do became suddenly clear. I realized I had gotten off track. It wasn't enough for me to discover my purpose; it was imperative that I put that purpose into action—consistently. Despite several interviews for some attractive positions, I withdrew my name from consideration.

For my next re-launch, I created a website, booked some public speaking engagements and began preliminary work on writing a book. I was comfortable with the public speaking portion of this new assignment and eager to dedicate to it on a full-time basis. However, the writing portion was a stretch for me. Nonetheless, purpose can only be fulfilled by the one equipped to do so—and destiny requires that you arrive alone, even if you rely on others along the way to help reach your destination. I needed to get the job done.

My mission was to inspire young people and old people, students and professionals, athletes and coaches, people who use wheelchairs and people who don't—to find, cultivate and live their purposes. I wanted to use my ability to connect with people, my communication skills and my unique life experiences to inspire, inform and instruct others to do the things they dreamed possible. People could benefit from my story and the sum total of lessons I've learned throughout it. It was time for my message to reach a wider audience.

By the fall of 2016, things were picking up. I was gaining traction on the speaker's circuit via social media, and I eventually landed a gig to speak at a national conference for bank educators through a speaker's bureau. If it went well, I'd leave there with bookings for the next year.

My first stop was on December 5, 2016 in Boston. I boarded a flight from Milwaukee to Boston, but about an hour and a half hour after takeoff, I found it challenging to breathe. I wore an oxygen mask the rest of the way and later learned a sub-massive blood clot had developed in my lungs.

I couldn't speak at the conference, and I eventually lost contact with the speaker's bureau. Once healthy, I had to start over—again. I had a few speaking gigs booked that spring and summer, but I had incurred some hefty medical expenses that needed to be paid off.

I accepted a temporary diversity position at Marquette University. I enjoyed working with the staff and students and attending their programs, but I soon realized this was not a long-term fit for me. Diversity had become a politically correct, hyper-sensitive subject, which meant that all efforts had to be qualified beforehand. I knew that my effectiveness in terms of fulfilling my purpose would be limited, which wouldn't be the best match for my natural gifts. The position offset my medical expenses, but I did not stay past the three-month period.

In April 2017, I addressed the freshman class at St. Thomas More High School in Milwaukee about servant leadership. After the presentation, one of the teachers approached me.

"Hey, Coach Cooks. Do you remember me?"

"No, I'm sorry, I don't."

"I was the last cut on JV my sophomore year at Marquette."

Oh, boy, I thought. I braced myself for a tongue lashing on how I'd ruined his high school experience, or how still now—many years later—he hasn't moved on from it.

"Eric Wolffersdorff," he said.

"Wolffersdorff? Yeah, I remember that name now."

"I still remember some of the things you said at basketball camp over ten years ago: 'You can only make a first impression once. Don't wind up on the short end of the court.'"

Like Tony Lang at the AAU tournament in St. Petersburg, Florida, it was another example of never knowing when someone else is listening or observing your character.

Eric had a prep period after lunch, so he, the campus minister (also a Marquette High grad), the assistant principal and I ate leftover pizza and shared updates and stories from our lives since our limited encounters several years ago. I told them about my near-death experience on the plane to Boston and my desire to write a book but that I wasn't sure I had the writing or organizational skills to get it done. I had an outline, but I was having trouble getting started with the writing. Eric spoke up.

"Well, I'm an English teacher."

A light bulb turned on. "You are?" I said. "Do you think you could help me out?"

"I've never actually published anything before, but I've always wanted to write a book. I'd be happy to help."

I gave him my business card with my contact information, and later that day he emailed and again offered his help. We met for many months after work, and I gave him newspaper and magazine articles, videos, podcasts, yearbooks, pictures—anything and everything that had ever been written or said about me. Eric came up with an outline very similar to mine, and he started writing—with me filling in details and stories. Once again, I was given what I needed when I needed it in order to move me forward with this process.

For the next ten months, Eric and I video-conferenced about once a week—brainstorming, organizing, reworking, and editing each other's work so it faithfully represented my mission. Thankfully, I persevered through the uncomfortable moments of writing—with the help of vinyl LPs from the days of "Morning Inspiration" willing me to the finish line.

EPILOGUE

THE LONGER I'VE BEEN IN A WHEELCHAIR, the more I've realized and appreciated how so many people like to go out of their way to help me. One of the things they often do is hold open doors for me. It's a great gesture, but what first-timers don't realize is that they first need to go all the way through the door, or else I'll roll over their feet. If they're halfway in-between, then neither of us is getting through the door. Their intentions are noble, but they don't do enough to help themselves first.

I like to think of this image as I ponder the essence of what servant leadership is all about. As humans, we have an inherent desire to help others—even strangers holding doors. But to make the intended impact, it takes more than just a spirit of altruism. It takes vision, experience and a keen understanding of how and why so that the act of service isn't merely an honorable thought but a constructive, empathetic action benefitting all parties. It often requires taking care of your business first—so that in a moment of need, you can help another without getting stuck in the doorway.

Servant leadership is all about changing others' experiences. Servant leaders are humble, action-minded individuals who work arm-in-arm with others and offer their footprints as models on the journey toward success. Many people are neither used to nor comfortable with that. It's not as cozy as telling others what to do. Telling people what to do and having people do what they ought to do are entirely different experiences. Action-based leaders hold everyone accountable—including themselves. And when it comes time for leaders to use their voices, they are clear, concise and consistent with their messages so everyone knows their roles, their goals and their returns. Words matter, and how well you package them and follow through with them matters even more. That's what leadership—and coaching—is all about.

The game of basketball has always been a microcosm for understanding my life and the world. It was how I made friends, settled disputes, built self-esteem and learned the value of team-work, commitment, discipline, toughness and collective responsibility. Basketball taught me the critical lesson of playing to my strengths and practicing my weaknesses until they became strengths. Good basketball players work on what's comfortable to them; great basketball players—just like great students, leaders and teachers—work on and reside in the domain of discomfort and pain.

A big part of basketball and life is learning how to navigate through difficult decisions and committing to something by making adjustments—not excuses. We all face life's challenges that force us to reinvent ourselves from time to time—to reflect, regroup and re-launch. Since experiencing my spinal aneurysm in 1979 and learning how to get undressed, I was driven by my goal of winning, getting home and restarting my life. I had to have the vision to see the ending from the beginning and commit to the necessary steps to see it all the way through. It took passion, patience and persistence, especially when the endgame seemed unattainable, but it became the muscle memory I stored away and retrieved when obstacles emerged.

Epilogue

Since that fateful day, my life hasn't been good...it's been great. It's still an unfolding, purposeful life that's driven by the next play. There's no telling what the future holds or where our next steps might lead us, and many things are completely out of our control. I've learned to put them in Jesus' hands and to just keep going—to never stop pursuing my passions. My relationship with Christ has served as the foundation of my life's story and has taken me From Paralysis to Purpose. 40 years after my commitment to Christ, my life has literally become a book—an outcome I never saw coming. God continues to bless me with the desires of my heart as His grace and wisdom assist me on my journey. My story continues beyond these pages.

The paradox of legacy is that destiny requires that we leave something behind—but we often can't see the effect of something while we're still here. We also can't force others around us to interpret our legacy the way we want. Life is too complicated and subjective for that.

My advice for others is the same I give myself: Worry about what you can control. Have the courage to confront your fears and uncertainties. Love in the face of mistreatment. Serve in the name of leadership. Remain steadfast in your beliefs about what is right and good in the world.

By doing this, people will remember you more for who you are and not just what you've done. Your character will take you where you need to go, and it will stay long after you're gone. Think about it. Practice it. Always keep the endgame in mind. That's the legacy I believe we all want to leave behind.

With the right attitude and perspective, getting undressed doesn't have to be a bad thing. It can help you go from your paralysis to uncovering and living your purpose.

About the Authors

David Cooks

David Cooks is the founder of David Cooks Enterprises, LLC, a speaking, coaching and training organization that helps businesses and individuals put their purpose into action. Rooted in servant leadership, David's experience as a coach, a businessman and an educator has equipped him to speak with clarity on teamwork, leadership and communication.

David received his Masters of Business Administration in Finance from Duke University and his Bachelor of Business Administration in Finance from the University of Wisconsin-Whitewater. His career path includes time spent in banking, education and athletics.

David is currently an assistant basketball coach at Concordia University in Mequon, Wisconsin. The highlights of David's coaching career are time spent at Duke University working with Hall of Fame coach Mike Krzyzewski and joining Frank Martin and Guy Rancourt in Estonia and Finland as a member of the coaching staff for USA East Coast Basketball.

David and his wife, MariPat, reside in Wauwatosa, Wisconsin.

Eric Wolffersdorff

Eric Wolffersdorff is a high school creative writing and English teacher at Burlington High School in Burlington, Wisconsin. As the final cut on the junior varsity basketball team at MUHS 14 years ago, he never played basketball under Coach Cooks' leadership—but through the writing of this book he feels he experienced part of the leadership he missed. After working together on this project, Eric feels he "made the cut" this time.

Eric received his Bachelor of Science degrees in Middle/Secondary Education and Writing Intensive English from Marquette University. Eric and his wife, Cassandra, live in Milwaukee, Wisconsin.

Discussion Questions

1. What are your takeaways from reading Getting Undressed?

2. What challenges in life could lead to a feeling of paralysis?

3. Who has been instrumental in helping you discover your purpose?

4. How does serving others help you deal with adversity?

5. What are the qualities of an effective leader?

6. What's the relationship between success and purpose?

INVITE DAVID COOKS TO SPEAK
TO YOUR COMPANY OR ORGANIZATION

David Cooks delivers a powerful message for young and old alike. With humor, insight, and perspective, David offers context as he explains what it takes to build a strong team and a winning culture within any organization and how *Getting Undressed* is an essential step in discovering one's purpose.

If you or your organization would like to book David Cooks, please contact him at: www.davidcooksspeaks.com

David Cooks
David Cooks Enterprises, LLC
P.O. Box 125
Butler, Wisconsin 53007
414-507-7677

CPSIA information can be obtained
at www.ICGtesting.com
Printed in the USA
FFHW011904171219
57038482-62633FF